THE ™
AND 1.   ﹏EL

A Victo﹏ ﹏ Murder

THEODORE DALRYMPLE

MONDAY BOOKS

A CIP catalogue record for this title is available from the British Library

ISBN: 978-1-906308-49-0

Typeset by Andrew Searle
Printed and bound by Cox and Wyman

www.mondaybooks.com
http://mondaybooks.wordpress.com/
info@mondaybooks.com

ACKNOWLEDGEMENTS

It is a pleasure to record my gratitude to the staff of the Public Library, St Helier, who demonstrated that the idea of public service is far from utopian. The new Jersey Archives have been criticised as clinical and soulless, but I found them admirably efficient and the staff extremely helpful.

I should like to thank the several researchers in Tasmania who answered questions quickly and selflessly.

The volunteers of the Lord Coutanche Library at the Société Jersiaise gave generously of their time and expertise.

Above all, I should like to thank Mrs Anna Baghiani, librarian to the Société, who found innumerable references for me, corrected many mistakes in Jersey history of a tyro such as I, and, in reading the manuscript, saved me from many foolish errors. She did far more to help me than any author has a right to ask librarians to do.

It goes without saying that remaining errors of fact or interpretation are my own.

Theodore Dalrymple

INTRODUCTION

To see a world in a grain of sand: few of us, surely, can never have experienced that semi-mystical state of mind enjoined by Blake. Who, even among the most hard-boiled materialists, has never looked closely at a tiny flower peeping almost blushingly from the undergrowth, or examined the marvellous contrivance of a crustacean's claw, and not felt that all is right with the world, that its beauty was somehow designed from the first for our particular delectation?

Likewise, the great historian, Sir Lewis Namier, said that in a drop of dew could be seen all the colours of the rainbow. By this he meant that in small events could be glimpsed the fundamental conditions, problems and dilemmas of human existence. This must be so, or much of the greatest literature would be a nullity.

But is murder a large or a small event? It depends, of course, upon the perspective employed. Nothing is large or small but thinking makes it so. The murder of a friend or relative is bound to loom large in anyone's life, even to the point of affecting the whole of its subsequent course; but in a world of war and revolution, of rapid social change and natural disaster, a single murder is but a pebble dropped into an ocean, soon forgotten however sensational it might have appeared at the time. Most murders never even reach public consciousness.

It is my belief, though, that human actions are never very far from deep, indeed the deepest, philosophical questions, either explicitly, or – more usually – implicitly. But if this is so, why have I taken murder *specifically* as my subject, my starting point? After all, if human actions are really never far from philosophical questions, why take murder rather than something more quotidian, say catching the bus?

The fact is that most of us (I include myself) are fascinated by murder. The reasons for this fascination are beyond my scope;

but it is so. And the attempt to eliminate prurience from human life would be far worse than the vice itself. Moreover, it would not work.

Second, why murders in Jersey, committed in 1845 and 1846, and long since forgotten? Jersey, one of the Channel Islands, is not a location synonymous with romance and fascination, such as Timbuktu or Bokhara. In my youth, Jersey was synonymous, rather, with milk, potatoes and pullovers: excellent products in their way, no doubt, but not such as to excite the imagination or set the pulse racing. Later, of course, Jersey became synonymous in my mind with bank accounts and tax havens (or, in the more graphic French phrase, *les paradis fiscales*); and a man whom I knew who worked as an undercover policeman told me that there was a lot of wickedness on Jersey. But the wickedness was of the convoluted financial variety, really understandable only to accountants, and not the type to spark our ever-prurient human interest.

One assumes that nothing much happens on Jersey; indeed, that nothing much has ever happened on Jersey, apart perhaps from the German occupation during the war (one of the longest in Europe). This is not quite so; there have been riots there, and in 1781 there was a Battle of Jersey – actually a mere skirmish, and over in 15 minutes, won by the British and commemorated in the famous painting by John Singleton Copley. And then, of course, there has been crime: for where there are humans, there is crime. One might almost say that crime is what distinguishes man from the animals, in that it requires *mens rea* to be committed, that is to say a guilty mind that animals cannot rise, or sink, to.

I have taken as my subject the murders of Thomas Hodge in December 1845, Simon Levi in January, 1846 and George Le Cronier in February 1846 only because they interested me; and they came to interest me quite by chance. I happened one day to walk through the Green Street Cemetery in St Helier, founded in 1827 and long since closed to new customers, except those whose families own a plot and are *bona fide* descendants of the residents; by far the grandest funerary monument in it was that of one George Le Cronier. It had a large and magnificent plinth, on which were four pillars supporting a cupola, which in turn sheltered a funerary urn. On the four sides of the plinth was the following inscription:

> George Le Cronier
> Centenier de la paroisse de St Hélier
>
> Cet honorable citoyen au moment ou il remplissait les devoirs de sa charge recu d'une main coupable une blessure mortelle
>
> Né le 30 mars 1793
> Decédé le 28 février 1846

Ses concitoyens voulant perpétuer leur régret et le souvenir de son dévouement ont fait ériger ce monument sur ces restes mortelles

> (George Le Cronier, Centenier[1], of the parish of St Helier. This honourable citizen received a mortal injury from a guilty hand while performing his official duty.
> Born 30 March, 1793, died 28 February, 1846. His fellow citizens, wanting to commemorate their regret and the memory of his devotion to his duty have erected this monument over his mortal remains.)

Ah, who can resist *une main coupable*? Certainly not I.

I conclude my preface by quoting another medical man who wrote about Jersey, Dr John Shebbeare:

Jersey is, indeed, of small contents, and not of numerous inhabitants; yet, many of the Grecian states, of whose actions Thucydides has given the history, were not so large... Whatever may prove to be the popular opinion of giving to the world the history of so small a state, I shall make no apology for the publication of the Narrative. To be of service to two and twenty thousand human beings[2], is an opportunity that seldom happens to a private man among the millions that live and die.[3]

My aims are more modest than those of Dr Shebbeare. If I succeed in interesting only a few Jerseymen[4] in episodes of their island's social history, I shall count myself sufficiently rewarded. He also serves who only stands and entertains.

I

On the morning of Sunday, 22 February, 1846, one of the *centeniers* of the parish of St Helier, George Le Cronier, aged nearly 53, and some of his officers, called on Mulberry Cottage, Patriotic Place. Mulberry Cottage was actually two cottages knocked into one, and still exists, though it has been renamed 'Sandringham House' and 'Rosedale', having been restored into two properties. Mulberry Cottage is the only building of its time to survive in Patriotic Place, the others having been knocked down and replaced by large modern buildings that overlook and dwarf them. Nearby, at the junction of Patriotic Place with Patriotic Street, stands a multi-storey car park. Despite its not altogether promising location, Mulberry Cottage, as was, is now worth over £1 million. In 1846, however, it was rented, not owner-occupied.

Despite its name, which is redolent of a village in the Cotswolds, Mulberry Cottage was what was in those days called *une maison de débauche*, or *une maison mal famée*, run by Mr and Mrs Le Gendre. Mrs Le Gendre also went by her maiden name, Marie Le Noble – a name that, as we shall see, somewhat belied her character.

M. *le Centenier* Le Cronier and his deputies caused 11 young women to be removed from thence and sent to the General Hospital, which was, despite its name, only partly a medical institution. It also served as an almshouse, poorhouse and house of correction.

The *Chronique de Jersey* for the following Wednesday was exultant:

> On Sunday morning the police went to Mulberry Cottage which they cleared out of prostitutes, numbering eleven, who were sent to the hospital. We can do no other than applaud this measure,

1

> which we would like to see extended to other such houses of ill-repute; and we hope that the Court will not hesitate to send back to their own country all those who are not native of this place, while sending those who are to the hospital and making them work there.[1]

I have been unable to discover whether any of these 11 were subsequently among the six *filles publiques* who 'on Friday early in the morning succeeded in escaping by making a hole in the wall below a window, and jumping over the walls around the building.'[2]

But it is probable that they were different prostitutes, for according to the diary of Sir John Le Couteur, in the Jersey Archives, for 27 March, 1846, 11 girls – 'the Seraglio from Mulberry Cottage' – appeared in court. 'It was dismal,' he writes, 'to see so many destitute Jersey creatures. Three were sisters. They were all to be sent to their parishes.'

Although a *centenier* was an unpaid officer, and a later eulogy of the murdered man described Jersey as 'her beloved Queen's paradise', Le Cronier's position was clearly not without its hazards. Not long before he met his death, he participated at a meeting of parishioners to re-elect another of the *centeniers* of St Helier, a M. Chevalier.

Chevalier had served three terms already, each of three years. He claimed, whether sincerely or not it is now impossible to say, that he did not want, for reasons of health and because he had other things to occupy him, to be re-elected. But he had been so popular in his post, said his colleague Le Cronier, that he would be elected anyhow – and he was, with only five votes against him. The chairman of the meeting said, 'There are a *centenier*'s duties that are painful for him to perform, and which can sometimes excite strong resentment. For example, if a person complains to a *centenier* that a man is mistreating his wife, he is forced to go there to prevent a possible murder; and by doing so, such a man could bear him eternal hatred; such things can happen in a town as populous [as St Helier].[3] (The population of the island was then about 50,000.[4])

George Le Cronier's life was to bear this out only too graphically; he was quite busy in his duties, and indeed had a surprisingly exciting life. There was one murder a month on Jersey, between December, 1845 and February, 1846; the last of them was his own.[5] On 13 December, 1845, the first of the three murders took place.

It came, said the *Chronique*, 'in a moment of madness, of true mental aberration', during which 'a man fatally struck one of his professional colleagues with his knife, following a fight that lasted only a few seconds!' As with many such killings, then and now, it was held to be as the result of 'the deplorable abuse of alcoholic liquor'.

A group of sailors from the crew of a ship, the *Syren*, were gathered in a boarding house run by one William le Gros. It was a Saturday night, and some members of the party were due to leave the following day; among them was Mr Thomas Hodge, mate of the *Syren*. The party, said the newspaper, was 'a kind of farewell dinner' in return for a birthday party he himself had thrown the previous Tuesday.

The evening had evidently gone well – 'The meal was gay and the conversation animated and expansive, although the guests did not in the slightest exceed the rules of sobriety' – when, some time between 9.30pm and 10pm, an outsider arrived. He was John Noon, the mate of the *Comus*, a ship that had arrived in port that day. He was also staying at M. Le Gros' lodgings, and 'came without invitation to sit down at the table of Hodge and his friends'. All might have been well, but for the looseness and coarseness of Noon's tongue. 'He soon addressed certain obscene words to Madame le Gros,' says the newspaper, 'causing indignation among the guests.'

3

They reprimanded him several times and asked him to leave, and when these entreaties proved fruitless they decided to get rid of their 'importunate' guest.

'Noon resisted, and was so aggressive that violence had to be used to restore the peace. Several punches were exchanged... In short, Hodge got up and showed him the door, but not without difficulty and a persistent struggle. Arriving on the stairs which led up to the house, Noon, furious at being thus treated, pulled his knife from his pocket and struck Hodge several times.'

Several of these blows were apparently superficial, but 'he struck once with such force that he penetrated his (Hodge's) flesh deeply, to the deep and upper part of his thigh where he opened, but did not sever, the femoral artery.'

Unsurprisingly, a 'most alarming haemorrhage' occurred – though, importantly, it was later recognised that a methodical application of pressure would have arrested the bleeding. Several people had gone to find the doctor, a man named Dickson, but in the interim no such pressure was applied to the wound and Hodge exsanguinated and died.

Perhaps unaware of the scale of the tragedy that had unfolded in his wake, Noon had 'retired aboard his ship, where he went to bed and was soon arrested by police officers'. He did not come quietly, however. The police officers making the arrest 'received the very valuable assistance of Mr Henry Smith, carpenter, a young man of Herculean strength, who had a dangerous struggle with Noon, for, in his state of frenetic excitement, this wretch tried to have recourse once more to his knife!'[6]

The following month, M. *le Centenier* le Cronier, who had evidently been one of the arresting officers, attended court to proffer evidence to the preliminary hearing. The arrest had been a violent one, he told the magistrates: Noon had attempted to bite the ear of one of his captors, and had been 'so violent that it was deemed necessary to tie his hands with rope.'[7]

Noon was eventually found guilty of manslaughter rather than of murder, his excellent defence advocate, Mr Hammond, arguing that his language in a company of sailors was not such as they would not have heard before; that he was provoked; that his victim had been pushing him down the stairs, which were of stone and therefore dangerous for him to fall down, so that there was an element of self-defence in what he did; and that he would have stabbed his victim somewhere else in the body if he had meant to kill him. Indeed, medical evidence had been called to the effect that the wound would not have been fatal if properly attended to.

'Anger,' said his advocate in his final peroration, 'is a brief madness, for where it takes over reason has ceased to rule. Is it possible to believe that half a minute could have given Noon sufficient time for reflection? The prisoner couldn't have wanted to commit the crime, and certainly not with premeditation.'

When, as a result of Hammond's pleading, Noon was found guilty of manslaughter, Hammond pushed his luck further and said that a year in prison would be sufficient to punish the crime; but Noon was sentenced to transportation to a penal colony for seven years.[8]

The night before Le Cronier's appearance in court on the Noon case had not been an entirely uneventful one for him; in fact, he had almost lost his life during it.

'The crump of an explosion' had been heard in the High Street at a quarter past nine, reported the *Chronique*. 'One might have thought it was the firing of a heavy artillery piece, or the collapse of a house. It was almost immediately followed by another explosion, less strong than the first.'

The people in that street stopped whatever they were doing and approached the place where the explosions came from. When they arrived they found a father and son – the Messrs. Preston – running from the building with their clothes in flames. 'Sharp cries were heard from the house where they worked,' writes the journalist. 'They came from the people who lived there, the flames preventing them from clearing a way to the street. Ladders were brought, and it was by this means that Mr Grandin *senior*, an infirm old man, and women and children, were extracted, though not without much difficulty. Mr Grandin was horribly burnt, and he was immediately taken to his son's house, where every possible medical assistance was given him.'

Among the people who were most actively engaged in this attempt to save the lives of those caught up in the explosion were M. *le Centenier* Le Cronier 'and two English gentlemen, whose names we have not been able to learn'. Le Cronier 'narrowly missed being killed when he fell down a trapdoor that was open but that he did not see, and he owed the preservation of his life to the help of the two gentlemen who were with him.'[9]

Mr Grandin died the following day, and the inquest[10] into his death found that the explosion had been caused by the Prestons, who were 'making fireworks in their shop.' Preston senior was melting some wax to make a fuse for a firework when a spark reached some gunpowder and then a whole barrel of it. (The other tenants didn't know that the Prestons stored gunpowder in the shop, and those who were insured found that their policies did not cover such accidents.) An acerbic little footnote to the report brings a smile to the face more than a century and a half later, but perhaps did not do so at the time:

> This is the third time Mr Preston senior has been injured in this manner. One might have thought that experience would have made him more circumspect when engaged in this kind of work, which is always dangerous; but it is quite otherwise.

As far as I have been able to ascertain, no action was ever taken against the Messrs Preston for their carelessness: at least, none was reported in the *Chronique*. These were the days before health and safety took the place of hope and charity; for while there was no action against the Prestons, there was an appeal to readers of the newspaper for funds for the Grandin family, which the Grandin family subsequently asked that no one should contribute to. Astonishingly for someone like me, a large city-dweller for much of my life, the explosion on Broad Street was not forgotten by a present day library volunteer of *la Société Jersiaise*[11], who told me that the dead Jean Grandin was the great-great-grandfather of a present inhabitant of the island. She even knew the precise location of the house in which the fire had taken place; for on a small island with a stable population of natives, the past is a graphically real participant in the present, with all the attendant advantages and disadvantages of such participation.

Of course, not all M. *le Centenier* Le Cronier's work was quite so dramatic or dangerous as on that fateful evening. Much of his work would seem to us trivial. One report has him placing an Elizabeth Roberts in the dock on the charge of having stolen a piece of cloth. Advocate Hammond, a busy man, spoke on her behalf. She admitted the offence, he said, but prayed the indulgence of the court. Unfortunately, she had been drunk when she committed the theft, and had not known what she was doing.

The asked-for indulgence was not forthcoming. The court sentenced her to six weeks in prison, and ordered that she should be in solitary confinement, on bread and water, for the last week.[12]

Le Cronier brought a man, Harry Perkins, before the court for having climbed into the home of a Mr Lymdon Poingdestre, at Mont-au-Prêtre, and where he had been found hiding in the coal cellar – possibly on an assignment of a romantic nature. M. *l'Avocat* Marett told the magistrates that the prisoner had not entered the house with the intention of theft, but only to talk to the domestic whom he knew there. 'He was talking to her when he heard Mr Poingdestre return, and he took refuge in the coal cellar so that she should not be reprimanded,' said the lawyer.

M. *le Procureur-Général* dismissed this excuse as inadmissible, because Perkins lived with his wife and children, and therefore ought not to have had secret interviews with Mr Poingdestre's domestic. Moreover, nothing justified a person entering another's house by climbing in at night.[13] Perkins was ordered to deposit five pounds with the court as an earnest of non-repetition of his behaviour.

Four days before his death, Le Cronier was involved in another domestic matter, when one John Stonebridge was arrested by him for having abandoned his wife and refused to maintain her, as well as his child. The man had arrived on the island a few days earlier from Guernsey, with his wife following shortly afterward – both of them having been required by judgment of the Court of Guernsey to leave that island, for reasons now lost, on pain of a £10 penalty.

On arrival on Jersey, Mrs Stonebridge had sought the *Centenier*'s help in bringing her apparently recalcitrant husband to heel, and Le Cronier had found him in a house in Don Street. When he refused the *Centenier*'s request that he fulfil his obligations towards the woman and child, he was taken immediately to prison, and the wife to the Hospital.

So far – for the times – so clear-cut. But the prisoner said in his defence that he had never lived with the woman, and that she in fact had a husband living. She replied that her husband had left for America about six years ago, and had since died.

Doubtless irritated by the intractability of the couple and uncertainty of the facts, M. *le Procureur-Général* ordered that they be sent back to Guernsey, so that the Court of that island might send them back to England at its own expense.[14]

Some matters were more serious. On the weekend before Le Cronier went to Mulberry Cottage for the first time, there had been violent trouble in St Helier to which he had been called.

Around midnight on the Saturday, and on into the early hours of the Sunday night, brawls broke out around the town between 'Irish workers and others', reported the *Chronique*. They had

8

started towards midnight in Conway Street, but peace was initially restored by M. Le Cronier, who had 'succeeded in separating the combatants' – a task, one imagines, not for the faint-hearted.

But his night's work was not done. 'At four in the morning,' says the newspaper, 'the fighters gathered at a house of ill-repute on the Parade, where they found several English workers who tried to keep them out of the house. A terrible fight started between them, and all that fell into their hands was used in both attack and defence; serious injuries followed.'

One man – a domestic servant of M. Jean Mourant, of the parish of St Saviour, 'was so badly injured that his life was put in danger; he is now recovering.'

The police arrested three of the brawlers and four *filles publiques* [prostitutes] who took part in the fight, and put them in prison. At the time of going to press, the police were scouring the town for the other participants.[15]

Violent squabbles seem to have been quite commonplace in St Helier and Le Cronier was often called upon to sort them out. Violence started young. One report speaks of an ugly battle between two boys aged between 12 and 13. During the fight, in the middle of King Street[16], 'one of the young *enragés* took out his knife and struck his adversary a violent blow with it. The wound was situated, we are told, near the twelfth rib on the right, and was an inch and a half deep. We don't know how serious it was, and the injured child was taken to his parents. As for the other, called Thomas West, he was seized by M. *le Centenier* Le Cronier and put in prison.[17]

Fighting was not the only misdemeanour committed by young boys. About a month before he was killed, Le Cronier apprehended and brought to court 'two young boys, whose names we did not catch, accused of having stolen some cod on the Chausée de St Helier.'[18] Because the parents of the boys, who had also been summoned to attend, failed to turn up, the case was adjourned, perhaps forever.

A further murder had taken place in St Helier in the very month before Le Cronier's own. Le Cronier was not directly involved in apprehending the culprit or in elucidating what happened, but his colleague and recently, and reluctantly, re-elected fellow-*centenier*, Chevalier, was. Moreover, the case had a bearing on the later response to Le Cronier's murder.

Under the heading *Horrible catastrophe*, the report in the *Chronique de Jersey*[1], detailed to the point of salacity but certainly recreating the atmosphere in a way that newspaper reports rarely do nowadays, wrote at length about the 'painful event' which 'has struck the population of the town with stupefaction and consternation'.

It had happened just before 2 a.m. at the Café Seward, in the Royal Square. The owner, John Seward, was enjoying a late-night game of cards, and doubtless a drink, around the fire with some friends – Messrs Simon Abraham, William Cock, John Bowdidge junior, Robert Jeffreys and John Gallie – when someone began knocking on the door. Seward tried to ignore the knocking, but it persisted. At length, he got up, went to the door and asked who it was. It was a John Nicolle – a hatter from nearby King Street. Seward opened the door. Nicolle entered with one William Martin, who happened to be an undertaker, and demanded a brandy and water. Given the lateness of the hour, Seward refused to serve them.

'On this,' the writer informs us, 'the said Mr Nicolle picked a quarrel with [Seward]; then he waved his fist and pulled at his clothes, and wanted him to come outside to fight. Hence, the said Mr Nicolle was not sober. The deponent pushed him outside, exchanged a few punches with him, chased him as far as the British Hotel, then returned.' Calm was thus re-established, and reigned for a quarter of an hour, until the confined space of the room rang to a mighty explosion – Seward later said he thought it was a cannon. One imagines that the company were stunned for a few moments, but on regaining their wits they saw Mr Abraham get up, groan and fall back injured.

Seward left the café immediately with Bowdidge, and they heard the steps of a man racing away as fast as he could through Peirson[2] Place to King Street; Seward thought, without being able either to see or identify him, that the man was Thomas Nicolle. Neighbours, aroused and no doubt startled by the noise of the gunshots, had come out and saw a woman who was running as if she wanted to join someone.

On their return to the café, Seward and Bowdidge found Mr Abraham already close to death; a domestic was bleeding profusely, having also been 'dangerously wounded' by 'two little bullets, one of which shattered her hand and the other of which entered her groin.'

Doctors were called, but they were unable to help Mr Abraham, other than to certify life extinct ('Mr Abraham,' writes the reporter with redundant emphasis, 'was dead, completely dead'). While they attended to the wounded woman, the police inspected the scene; this disclosed that the barrel of a gun had been applied close to the shutter, 'which was holed by eight little shots. The Royal Square was full the whole day long with people wanting to know the details of this awful affair.'

They went to Thomas Nicolle's home and arrested him.

With commendable speed, the inquest opened in the Café Seward at one o'clock the following day.

The body of Mr Abraham was identified by Messrs. Simeon Jewell and Samuel Marks as being that of Simon Levi, who went under the name of Abraham because he worked in his brother-in-law's business, Abraham and Company. Levi was about 60 years old, and had been born (surely unusually for a Jew at the time) in Lyme Regis in Dorset.

John Seward outlined the events as he had seen them, and 'Dr Dickson, junior', having examined the body of the unfortunate Mr Abraham, explained that a bullet had entered his back and exited

11

through his abdomen. Although this was 'certainly the cause of death, he nevertheless recommended a post mortem, which he subsequently was asked to perform with two other doctors (one of whom, in the event, was his father).'

Robert Jeffreys told the inquest that he had changed places with the deceased shortly before the shooting, a trivial and seemingly inconsequential action which had saved his life.

There were further revelations on subsequent days. Chevalier went to Nicolle's house and knocked on the door. Nicolle opened it, and then shut it and locked it again. Chevalier was dissuaded by onlookers from making a forced entry because it was thought that Nicolle had guns and was still in a state of excitement.[3] A guard was therefore kept on Nicolle's house until the following morning, when the kitchen door was found to be open. Going upstairs, Chevalier found Nicolle in his room with a child in his arms. The child was removed from him, and Chevalier said, in an attempt to trap him into a confession, 'You've made a pretty job of it, you have shattered Mr Seward's shutters.'[4] But Nicolle played dumb and claimed not to know what Chevalier was talking about, and likewise said that he possessed no guns, although two were soon found in his room, one of them recently discharged (confirmed by an armourer of St Helier who was asked his opinion), as well as an axe behind the door. He was arrested and taken to prison.

Some of the testimony gathered by the preliminary court hearings was informative about more than just the case to someone reading it more than a century and a half later. John Weston was employed as a watchman to make sure that no one fell down the sewer at night in Church Lane: though whether his position was permanent or temporary was not worthy of mention. St Helier – no giant metropolis, after all – was therefore unlikely to have been sweet-smelling at that epoch.

Weston testified that shortly before the shooting he had heard noise in Library Place. 'He went there immediately, and saw Mr Thomas Nicolle stretched out on the ground. Nicolle told him that Mr Seward had just knocked him over. The deponent asked the latter to desist, which he did and withdrew. He asked the said Nicolle to return home, and in so doing the latter said, 'I'll give him a good lesson!'[5]

This, if believed, was good evidence of premeditation, of course.

Three days after Abraham, or Levi, was shot, Miss Cook discovered a third wound, suggesting, perhaps, that she did not undress each day. The newspaper informed its readers:

> Miss Cook, who has suffered greatly from her wounds, is now considered out of danger. On Monday evening, she noticed a black stripe on her left side, and on examining her corset, Dr Dickson, junior, discovered that she had been struck by a third bullet in the direction of the heart. It was probably to the thickness of her corset and her clothes that she owes her survival.[6]

Later investigation found the underlying reason for the quarrel between Seward and Nicolle. The latter objected to a bill for six shillings for two bottles of champagne that he claimed never to have had, though there is no doubt that champagne was one of his tipples, for he had drunk some in another café that very evening.[7]

Witness depositions continued for a month. Nicolle called his neighbour, John Hunt, who deposed that Nicolle used his guns for shooting rats and the ave for chopping wood. He had known the prisoner for nine years, four of them more intimately. He had always found him just, honest and well-behaved; but over the last six to eight months, he believed, from his appearance, that he was not fully in control of his faculties. After a conversation with Nicolle's wife, who told him that her husband had suffered from a fever, he had observed him more closely. He had seen him enter his room and throw his tools and his belongings out of the window for no reason; he had seen him open his window and shoot at chimney pots; and when he spoke to him about important matters, he would go off at a complete tangent and could not sustain a conversation.[8]

Also called as a witness to his mental condition was Mrs Sophia Hodder, an inhabitant of Guernsey. Nicolle had lived on Guernsey for 20 months, learning his trade as a hatter with Mrs Hodder and her husband. According to her, his behaviour appeared strange and completely inexplicable on a number of occasions. For example, she had seen him beating the walls with his fists until they bled, as if he were fighting someone. She said to him, 'You're mad again, Thomas!' to which he replied 'It's all right, do you see it, it is a bullet!' He had also threatened to shoot a girl with whom he had just gone for a walk; Mrs Hodder found him in his room with his gun and sharpening his flint preparatory to doing so. Once she found him squatting in a corner of his room, and she called him 'Mad fool!' whereupon he inscribed those words on the top of his door and objected strongly to their removal. One night he slept in a box in his room instead of in his bed. Mrs Hodder had never seen him drunk, and said that he was known on the island as 'Mad Nicolle.'[9]

However, Nicolle was not so permanently mad that he was unable to place the following advertisement in the *Jersey Herald*, six months before he committed his murder, on June 13, 1845:

> T. Nicolle having lately visited London and Paris, is returned with a choice selection of *Beaver*, *Silk* and short nap *Paris hats*, not to be equalled in any warehouse in the Island; selected from the different first rate warehouses in both Towns. The *Proteus*, *Templar*, *Bonnet* and *Ladies Night Templar Caps* in all varieties.
> Childrens' and other Fancy Caps sold at unequalled Low Prices.

Superior Paris Ventilating Hats, with Velvet Under
Brims and Quilted Linings of the most Modern
Shapes.
Persons desirous of obtaining a good and desirable
article at a moderate rate are desired to call at
Thomas Nicolle's Hat and Cap Warehouse.

Few people desirous of obtaining a good and desirable article
realised that they were doing so from a future murderer. We
understand life backwards but live it forwards.

The advocate for the defence, once again the excellent Mr
Hammond, first drew attention to the merely circumstantial
evidence against his client; but if it were accepted that he had
done the act (and the evidence that he had was very strong, as
Mr Hammond must have known), then he was not guilty of
murder, first, because he had never intended to kill Mr Abraham,
against whom he had no quarrel; and, second, on account of his
mental condition, which both his neighbour and Mrs Hodder had
testified to. Mr Hammond had recourse to the words of Pinel,
the great French alienist, who argued that if a man suffered from
monomania he might carry on his business as normal, apparently
with good sense, and yet be so mad that he was not responsible for
a criminal act.

The *Procureur-Général* argued against this. Surely the fact that
he was drunk, that he had had a quarrel over a bill, that he had
indicated quite clearly his intention to return to the Café Seward
and cause damage, that he was able to carry on his normal business
notwithstanding occasional eccentricities (and Mrs Hodder's
testimony referred to a period nine years before), indicated that he
was guilty of murder?

The jury sided with the *Procureur-Général* and found Nicolle
guilty – the formula of the verdict in Jersey law, strange to modern
ears, being 'more guilty than innocent.' At 11 o'clock at night,
there having been an adjournment for refreshments at 6.20 p.m.,

in the middle of Mr Hammond's final address, he was sentenced to death.[10]

He was to be executed within three weeks of sentence having been passed.

On pronouncing sentence, the Bailiff of Jersey (the Chief Justice of the Island, among other things) said what surely could have been said to thousands of other criminals, before and since:

> Thomas Nicolle, if instead of having passed your time in taverns and other places of debauchery, you had tried to fulfil duties as a citizen, son, husband and father, you would not now be dishonouring the beings to whom you gave existence.

And he added what will appear to the reader, according to taste, either deeply compassionate or unctuously hypocritical:

> I do not make these observations in order to add to the anxieties that you must now be feeling; I ask you to use the little time you have left on earth in prayer and supplication at the foot of the throne of Divine Grace...

Mr Hammond did not rely on Divine Grace alone; he went to England, 'with dossiers and petitions', to ask the Tory Home Secretary, Sir James Graham, to reprieve Nicolle.

The days passed, and the condemned man and his wife had what they believed to be a last meeting. It seems unlikely that the *Chronique de Jersey* was present, but it was able, somehow, to inform its readers of the solemnity of the occasion. 'It was deeply painful,' reported the newspaper. 'These two unhappy persons could not pronounce a single word. All Mrs Nicolle could say on leaving her husband was "God bless you." She was conducted to prison, and returned home, in a vehicle, her health giving rise to great anxiety.[11]

On 7 April, however, news of commutation was received. Advocate Hammond had been successful with Sir James Graham; he sent a message, by means of 'electric telegraph', to Southampton (undersea cables were not laid until 1858), asking the harbour-master unfailingly to ensure that it was put on the packet to Jersey, so that the Nicolle family should learn the good news as soon as possible.[12] Hammond feared that his letter to the condemned man's wife, following by normal post, would delay matters.

Nicolle was to be transported 'for the term of his natural life' to New South Wales, Van Diemen's Land or 'one of the adjacent isles,' rather than be executed. The commutation of sentence was ordered on three grounds: first, that there had been a fight, and therefore (presumably) it was believed that there was an element of provocation in the situation; second, that Nicolle had been in a state of unusual excitation; and, third, that there was the suggestion of 'mental alienation,' that is to say madness, in his case.

The reprieve was, of course, given in the name of Queen Victoria, and the *Chronique de Jersey* was extremely pleased by it:

> This merciful act of our debonair sovereign has caused a general satisfaction in the country, where it is very rarely that public executions have taken place.[13]

The idea of Victoria as 'debonair' surprises us, whose mental image of the Queen is of a portly and terminally unamused widow; and also the expression 'in the country' reminds us how different from the English, Scottish, Welsh and Irish the inhabitants of Jersey thought (and still think) themselves.

The killing of Le Cronier was later to arouse very different emotions in the heart of the *Chronique de Jersey*.

17

Another Jersey newspaper, *Le Constitutionnel*, used the killing of Thomas Hodge to excoriate the elective volunteer police system of the island, against which it lost no opportunity to rail, demanding a professional force in place of the amateur. The *Chronique de Jersey*, to the contrary, supported the system and wanted to keep it intact.

The rivalry between the newspapers was intense. Perhaps this is not altogether surprising since, by the 1830s, there were 11 of them on the island[14], one for roughly every four thousand persons, or for every two thousand literate adults, and in 1846 there were still at least eight.[15] Competition was fierce and unconstrained, red in tooth and claw. As we shall see, the editors wrote about each other with a freedom (that is to say, a licence to insult) that makes the worst of our tabloids today seem genteel, even lady-like. Indeed, *The Sun* is more like *The Lady* than it is like *Le Constitutionnel*.

III

One might have supposed that Mr Seward, the owner of the
café bearing his name, would seek a quiet life after the 'horrible
catastrophe' that had recently taken place in it, but very much to
the contrary: he was obviously a man of undaunted spirit. One
month later the *Chronique de Jersey* gleefully reported an altercation
between Seward and Abraham Jones Le Cras, the editor of a rival
newspaper, the *Jersey and Guernsey News*.

'The American method of pursuing editors was put into
practice yesterday in St Helier,' reported the *Chronique*, going on
to explain that there had been a 'skirmish' after Seward had taken
offence at an article published by Le Cras. Le Cras' error had
been to write an article 'about the present state of inns of Jersey',
and to apply the epithet 'gambling' to Mr Seward's café.

According to the journalist, Seward took this very badly, and
'wandered the streets of the town for two days, looking for the
unfortunate editor.' He finally caught him near the office of the
News, 'but whether by chance or design the Editor escaped scot-
free that day.'

But he was not able to evade his nemesis forever. 'On Monday,
Seward stood guard once more and ventured so far as to insinuate
himself, whip in hand, into the sanctuary of the man of letters. The
latter having been warned, his door to his room was firmly locked,
and Mr Seward could not gain entry. However, the offended man
did not accept defeat, and after several of the Editor's efforts to
escape, it seemed that the instrument of vengeance gained new
strength in the hands of the former.'

When Seward's attention wandered, presumably, Le Cras
managed to make a run for it – 'accompanied by a friend, making
the best use possible of his legs, going in the direction of his home.'
One imagines him chortling at having outwitted his opponent, but
if he did so then his joy was temporary.

19

'Congratulating himself on the advantage he had gained on his adversary, (he) turned into Cattle Street, (but) who should attract his attention but the terrible Mr Seward! There was not a moment to lose, the Editor effectuated a quick retreat, but not successfully before Mr Seward applied his iron grip to his shoulders. The Editor took refuge in a nearby shop, followed by Mr Seward, who dealt him several blows with his whip; punches were then exchanged between them, and Mr Seward, believing that he had taken his revenge, abandoned the field of battle. Mr Le Cras was soon accompanied home by a police officer, and is now a little "the worse for wear[1]" as a result of the blows he received.'

It is difficult not to detect delight in this facetious account, rather than sympathy or solidarity with a colleague of the press.

Not surprisingly, Seward's attack on Le Cras soon gave rise to a court case. Mr Le Cras asked the court to indict Seward, and it agreed to do so by a vote of two judges to one.[2] Two weeks later, the case began to be heard in the Royal Court. Mr Advocate Marett, appearing for the defendant, played down the seriousness of the altercation. Instead of being gravely maltreated, he told the court, the complainant had 'received only a few light blows of a riding crop', which the defendant had administered because of the 'continual attacks' directed at him by the newspaperman. What had happened in Mr Seward's house was already unfortunate enough, without anyone trying to ruin him into the bargain.

Le Cras had 'tried to take the bread from out of his mouth' and 'tried to make the public believe that his house was a disorderly one of debauchery', asserted the lawyer.

The *Chronique* report says that, here 'Mr Marett read out the articles in which Mr Le Cras used words such as *loose café, haunt of dissipation*[3], etc.) Having heard such calumnies, was there not enough to justify Mr Seward's conduct? It was said that the Café Seward closed very late; but why should he not be allowed to keep his friend till two in the morning, when establishments frequented by the upper class and the nobility stayed open until that hour?'

Mr Le Cras had sought to ruin Mr Seward by means of newspaper articles, said the lawyer. Now he wanted to do it by means of a long and costly trial. To avoid this, the defendant admitted the facts in the accusation; but he had been provoked by the complainant, who had insulted him in his newspaper to bring about his ruin.

Le Cras' advocate, Mr Godfray, did not agree. He refuted the contention that his articles in the *News* had damaged the defendant or had threatened his total ruin. The articles did not justify the conduct of the defendant who, moreover, could have complained to the Court rather than taken justice into his own hands.

Importantly, from the point of view of future developments, when Mr Le Cras complained about the conduct of the police in the case, some people in the court, including two of the judges, began to laugh.[4]

The court met again two weeks later. Mr Advocate Godfray said that, since the defendant had admitted all the facts of the case, he was going to confine himself to establishing that the plaintiff had the right to claim the amount he had asked for – £100, or about £10,000 in today's money (and soon, no doubt, to be much more than that). His client was an old man – born in 1798, Le Cras was then 48, which, no doubt, counted as 'old' at a time when average life expectancy was 45 – while his adversary was a man at the height of his powers (he was 30). Had Seward faced an adversary of his own age and strength, said Godfray, he would never have taken the law into his own hands. Furthermore, Le Cras had only reprinted, word for word, an article that had already appeared in another newspaper, the *Jersey Times*, the same week. Mr Seward should have been the last person to commit an assault, in view of the unfortunate events at his house, for which a man, Nicolle, was still under sentence of death, said Godfray.

In reply, Mr Marett, for Mr Seward, said that Mr Godfray had tried to make the whole affair appear as though it were serious; but what, he asked, had really taken place? M. Le Cras had thought fit to publish calumnies against his client and sought thereby to ruin him, and in exchange had received several light blows with the hand of a whip to punish him, and to demonstrate Seward's contempt for him to the public. Mr Godfray had said that Seward should have been the last person to commit an assault after what had happened in his café; but assuredly Mr A J Le Cras should have been the last one to write libels, because his own advocate, Mr Godfray, having been called a 'humbug' by him in print, had once demanded £500 (£50,000 in today's money) in damages from him, and there had not been much difference between the two instances of libel. In fact, the character of Seward had been worse traduced than that of Mr Godfray. Marett concluded by hoping that the court would award only nominal damages, in order to show how reprehensible Mr Le Cras' conduct had been.

The court was agreed that, irrespective of the provocation offered by Le Cras, Seward should not have behaved as he did, and fined him £10. But the judges were divided as to the damages to be paid to Le Cras, whether they should be nominal or punitive. One thought he should receive £10, another one shilling. The third judge, with the casting vote, decided on £10, but it is unlikely that Le Cras ever succeeded in extracting it from his adversary, for Seward immediately entered an appeal and appeals dragged on for years.

IV

Biographical dictionaries usually begin their brief lives by giving in one word a subject's principal field of activity or claim to fame: doctor, scientist, writer, painter and so forth. The entry for Abraham Jones Le Cras (1798 – 1869) styles him as 'Agitator.'[1]

In fact he was far more than this might suggest. He was born in England of Jersey stock, and he returned to Jersey at some time in his childhood or adolescence. He first came to prominence on the island as a vendor of patent medicines, for example *Stomachic Candy*, *Medicinal Snuff*, *Pectoral Pills* and (apparently his best-seller) *Essence of Life*, advertised as 'the most universal remedy known.'

Le Cras then founded his own newspaper, the *Jersey and Guernsey News*, and became a campaigning journalist.[2] According to The Newspaper Press Directory of 1846, this newspaper 'advocates the removal of restrictions on commerce, the advancement of education, and encouragement of science, the free toleration of all religions, and is partial to Dissenters; seeks a reform of the abuses of the peculiar laws of the island, which are the old Norman, and the mode they are administered in; urges the necessity of adoption of the English language [in Jersey, where a form of French was still predominant]...'

By this time, Le Cras had become a Swedenborgian, producing a tract entitled *On The Philosophy Of A Divine Revelation, By Means Of Inspired Writings; And Of "God Manifest in the Flesh", in the Person of Our Lord and Saviour Jesus Christ: Being an Humble Attempt to Account for the Apparent Discrepancies and Contradictions in the Literal Sense of the Word, and of Those Infirmities and Frailties.* This modest little work, published in 1844, when Le Cras was editor of the *Jersey and Guernsey News*, attempts to reconcile what he saw as inconsistencies in the New Testament by means of Swedenborgian philosophy. Whatever the theological value of the book, printed at the News Office in Jersey, but sold by Newbury of Holborn, Hodson of Fleet Street, Galignant of Paris, Wiley and Putman of New York, Otis Clapp of Boston, Peck of Buffalo, and Morgan of Cincinnati, it starts with a principle that has its dangers as far as society and the enforcement of the criminal law are concerned. Le Cras begins:

> The necessity of a just discrimination of realities from appearances, has long been considered by the learned as a matter of the first importance, inasmuch as the prosperity of the sciences greatly depends thereon...

True enough, no doubt; for if immediate appearance were all there were to reality, there would be no need to investigate anything more deeply (though whether we ever penetrate behind appearances to reality itself is a question with which philosophers have wrestled manfully but unavailingly for centuries, or millennia). Speaking of human action, however, Le Cras develops a doctrine that is potentially dangerous:

> The appearance here spoken of, is man's external life, which unless it flows spontaneously from his internal state, so as to become a true index to it, or exact effigy of it, is a fallacious criterion to form our judgment upon... We ought to judge more by his motives than his actions – or, to speak logically, we ought to look more into the intentions of his mind, because that flows freely from his inward state.[3]

This seems perilously close to the modern doctrine of *the real me*, that is to say the immaculate person within who exists independently of all he does and remains intact whatever he does. The sadistic murderer thus insists that his action was not *really* his, but that of a temporary quasi-physiological aberration; the drunkard (when he learns that he has done something terrible) that it was the alcohol, and not he, that was 'talking.'

A clue, perhaps, to Abraham Jones Le Cras' character can be found in the following passage:

> The experience of all those who are gifted with reflection, demonstrates, that the perceptions of man when he becomes truly rational, are decidedly opposite or contrary to those which he had in a sensual state...[4]

A man who believes this is, I think, unlikely to be a conformist in religion or in anything else, to accept something as true merely because millions of people have accepted it before him. He is unlikely to adhere to any church that he did not found himself, and is quite likely to suppose that the truth of his ideas is proportional to the opposition that they arouse. Le Cras did, in fact, found a church in St Helier – the New Church on Victoria Street, consecrated 8 April, 1849, and recently sold for secular purposes.

But Abraham Jones Le Cras' greatest concern, not to say his obsession, was not religious truth, but to Anglicise Jersey, both as to its language and institutions. He lived at a time of change, which he did everything in his power to bring about or quicken. His *magnum opus* is the memorably titled *The Constitution of Jersey, Shewing Its Incorporation with the Kingdom of England by Henry Ist, the Legislative Powers of Parliament, and the Nature of the Authority of the Queen in Council over the said Island: Observations on the Institution of the Royal Court, Composed of Bailly and Twelve Jurats: Its Power, both Judicial and Political; the Duties and Responsibilities of the Lieutenant Governor and other Public Officers; the Enlargement of the said Court, by the Incorporation of the Rectors, so as to Constitute it of the Three Estates as a Body of Civil Justice and Government or Common Council of the Isle.* Concision was not one of Le Cras' virtues.

The tendency of this work (as of several others) was to show that, contrary to the self-flattering opinion of Jerseymen, the supposed autonomy of Jersey was based upon legal misconception and fraud; that, legally speaking, Jersey was and had always been under direct English jurisdiction. Le Cras wanted the court of Jersey to become part of the Hampshire Circuit, just as, in Church of England administration, it was part of the Diocese of Winchester. Written at the high tide of English optimism about themselves, not to say complacency and arrogance, when England seemed to be the new middle kingdom, Le Cras saw all things English as inherently and almost *ipso facto* superior to all others. Le Cras' historical work, obsessively detailed, is now dismissed as being irredeemably tendentious, like the researches of those enthusiasts who tried to prove that the British, or the Mayans of Central America, were the lost tribe of Israel. And indeed, when one looks at the books that formerly belonged to him, now in the Lord Coutanche Library of the *Société Jersiaise*, one can see by his underlinings and annotations that he is not seeking truth but looking for confirmation of his predetermined views.

Jersey was indeed changing rapidly while Le Cras wrote. By 1851, 12,000 of its 51,000 inhabitants were recent English immigrants, of whom 41 per cent were artisans, 38 per cent were labourers, 7 per cent were professionals or traders, and 14 per cent were people of independent means.[5] The latter were, of course, *la crème de la crème* of Jersey society – at least in their own opinion. They were retirees, come to Jersey because of its relatively mild climate and cheap cost of living. Their principal problem, according to one observer, was 'to get quit of time,' in other words boredom.[6] For this purpose, they arranged an endless round of balls and other entertainments.

Somewhat surprisingly, at least to me, was the fact that Jersey was even then a highly urbanised society; 50 to 60 per cent of the population – some 25,000 to 30,000 people – lived in the capital, St Helier, and 7,000 of the English immigrants lived there, spreading the English language and demanding equal rights for it. By 1850, in fact, English was the predominant language in St Helier.

Elsewhere, a form of Norman French, *Jerrias*, was the main language.[7] It was among Le Cras' many complaints that Jersey Legal French was the language still used in court, no sworn interpreter being used. Two years before these events, an English lawyer resident on the island, a 6ft 10in giant of a man called Charles Carus Wilson, was sentenced to imprisonment in Jersey for refusing to speak French in court and insisting upon English.

Le Cras was an inveterate petitioner. He petitioned Lord Melbourne, Lord John Russell, Sir James Graham and Sir George Grey in an attempt to right the various injustices he thought British residents of Jersey suffered, who paid local taxes but were denied any influence in local affairs. When they fell on hard times, and needed the charitable support from the parish, they were simply deported, no matter how many years they might have contributed previously through taxes to pay for parish relief of others. This, said Le Cras, was grossly unjust; if he were writing now, he would call it discriminatory.

In 1845, Le Cras petitioned the government in London that English law be adopted in Jersey lock, stock and barrel.

The situation, he thought, was a classic case of old political forms not keeping pace with new demographic and economic realities. Le Cras retained his faith in the absolute superiority of British over traditional forms of government even when his first petition, presented in 1832, had not been answered more than five years later, despite an acknowledgement of receipt, and his reminder to Lord Melbourne's successor.[8] His letters were always logical, but nevertheless had the distinct whiff of the querulant about them. They were written in a fine, spidery, micrographic hand of the kind with which lunatic asylum artists used to adorn their artwork.[9]

Le Cras founded the *British Protection Society* to protect the rights of British immigrants on the island. He was exercised not only about the legal system but about the system of policing on the island. The householders of each parish on the island (of which there were, and are, 12) elected an honorary *Connétable*, or Constable, who was not only head of police for the parish, but sat in the island's legislature. Under him in the hierarchy were the elected *centeniers*, socially always a cut below the *Connétable*, numbering four in St Helier, and then the *vingteniers*, numbering seven in St Helier. Originally, the *centenier* and *vingteniers*, who were paid nothing, were responsible for keeping order in areas of 120 households, though, with the growth of population, this system could not, of course, be maintained unaltered. They nevertheless continued to be responsible for defined geographical areas, and indeed had no legal powers beyond those areas, except in cases of *flagrant délit*. Beneath the *vingteniers* came the petty constables, of whom St Helier at the time rejoiced in 24.

According to Le Cras, the manner in which the *connétables*, *centeniers* and *vingteniers* were elected was corrupt and arbitrary. There was no electoral list; the police, who were themselves allowed to vote in all parish assemblies, simply allowed people into the meetings according to their political sympathies. Anyone who was likely to vote against the current police was excluded.[10] Moreover, the ballot was not a secret one; everyone knew who everyone had voted for.

If what Le Cras said was true, it was obviously a system ripe for abuse; and certainly elections without opposition, or in which more than 99 per cent of the votes are cast for the incumbent smack of totalitarianism or African post-colonialism. In the re-election in 1845 of the *Connétable* of St Helier, for example, a M. Le Sueur was re-elected by 572 votes to none, there being no opponent; and this 'despite all the intrigues, calumnies, and invective of the thousand and one correspondents of the *Bien public* [the subtitle of the *Constitutionnel* being '*Le Journal du bien public*' – 'The Journal of the Public Good' – a self-awarded sobriquet that its opponents often used with irony or sarcasm], who, for six months, have stated

28

in the most positive manner that M. Le Sueur had lost the little popularity that he had ever had.'[11]

Not quite every election on the island was like that of M. Le Sueur, however. The results of the election for the *centenier* of the parish of St Peter in 1846, for example, were as follows:

For M. Dumaresq (the incumbent) 108
For M. Balleine 94[12]

But there was another source of corruption in the system. The position of policeman being an honorary one, they had to earn their living another way, usually as small tradesmen. Le Cras' British Protection Society published the names of their businesses so that British residents, who were excluded from voting in the elections for the police, might boycott them. Even worse, some of the policemen were wine and spirit merchants; they were also in charge of giving licences to inns and taverns. Not surprisingly, they were quite lax in this matter; according to Le Cras there were 500 licensed 'public houses and places of debauchery' in St Helier, one for every 50 or 60 people, that is to say for every 25 or 30 adults. 'This,' he wrote, in one of his petitions to London, 'is not only calculated to have a demoralising effect on the population, but is actually causing an alarming increase of crime, as may be witnessed by the fact that no less than three murders were committed in the town parish in the last weeks.'[13] Indeed, such corruption had played its part in the murder of the unfortunate Mr Levi. Mr Beward was permitted by the police to open late at night because one of their number supplied him with his wine and spirits. If it had not been for the late opening, according to Le Cras, it is more than likely that the murder would not have happened. Everyone would have been safely tucked up in bed.

Nor was this all. The café-owner Seward was protected by the police when he beat Le Cras, at least according to Le Cras himself. A few months after the three murders took place, there was a Royal Commission in Jersey to enquire into the criminal law of the island, largely in response to the agitation of Le Cras and others. Le Cras deposed to the Commission that he had got wind of Seward's intention to beat him before he did so, and had written to the police, in the person of *Centenier* Duparq (elsewhere spelled 'Du Parc'), to request him to bind over Seward to keep the peace, as he was empowered to do, but which he did not do.[14]

Furthermore, when the man who was accompanying Le Cras when he was assaulted by Seward, a jeweller by the name of John Sullivan, ran to fetch a policeman, the *Vingtenier* Mahy who lived nearby, the latter flatly refused to come to his assistance. Sullivan was questioned by the Royal Commission:

> Q: It had been a violent assault, had it?
>
> A: A very violent assault.
>
> Q: Upon making the complaint, will you tell us what Mr. Mahy said?
>
> A: Upon that Mr. Mahy said that he would not move on any account.
>
> Q: Did he give any reason why?
>
> A: He said that Mr. Le Cras called the police 'illiterate Policemen' and then came to them for assistance. I did all I could to persuade him to come. He still persisted in saying that he would not.

The Commission then asked a question that showed that they took Le Cras' allegations seriously:

> Q: What is Mr. Mahy?
>
> A: A wine and spirit merchant.[15]

The *Centenier* Duparq was questioned by the Commission:

30

A: On receiving the letter of Mr Le Cras, I went with the party [who delivered the letter] to Mr Seward; but he was not at home. I also went again with my son, who was a police officer.

Q: You did not find him at home?

A: No.

Q: Was your only reason for not taking this security [for Seward to keep the peace] not finding Mr. Seward at home?

A: That was my only reason.

Q: You did not make any subsequent enquiry?

A: No. I was called away, after that, on another police business.

Q: How far have you to go to Mr Seward's?

A: About four or five hundred yards.

Q: What is your business?

A: I am a wine and spirit merchant.

At this point, Le Cras, who was obviously present, burst in: 'Mr Seward keeps a public house.' Duparq then denied that he had ever had any business dealings with Seward.[16]

The *Connétable* of St Helier, Pierre (or Peter) le Sueur, he who had been re-elected unanimously the year before, was examined on the matter by the Commission, and had three lines of defence.[17] In support of the *Vingtenier* Mahy, one of his officers, he said what was not, and could not have been true, that Mahy thought that by the time Sullivan reached him the assault was over; and that this being the case, and the events being outside his *vingtaine*, the matter was no longer one of *flagrant délit*, and therefore none of his business. But this was clearly a bogus excuse, as well as contrary to Sullivan's evidence, for Sullivan stated that Mahy gave quite another reason for refusing to act, namely Le Cras's hostility to the police. Moreover, he could not have known, sitting in his own house, that the assault *was* over, and was not a continuing *flagrant délit*.

But the *Connétable*'s second line of defence was more convincing. He said that when Le Cras brought a complaint to him, he agreed to lay charges against Seward, but before he was able to do so Le Cras had already brought an action *en adjonction*, what in effect is a private prosecution. It was therefore pointless for him to continue with an official prosecution. Since Le Cras in fact lost little time in bringing his private prosecution, four days, Le Sueur's explanation might be correct – unless one believes that if a man lies about one thing, he must be a liar about another.

His third line of defence was to cast doubt on Le Cras's dependability as a witness. He told the Commission that this was not the first complaint he had had from Le Cras, and produced two letters written to him by the newspaper editor in 1842. The letters alleged that Le Cras and his son had each 'been murderously assaulted in the public market', and requested that the policeman bind the guilty party to keep the peace, 'and also to take measures to cause him to be dealt with according to law.'

The Commissioners continued:

> Q: What way do you use these letters?
> A: Mr. Le Cras had been assaulted, on account, of course, of an article which appeared in his paper, by Mr. Du Jardin. He complained of having been murderously assaulted, when a whip had been used. I suppose it was more to shew his contempt of the person than anything else.
> Q: You introduce these letters to shew that Mr. Le Cras takes a rather exaggerated view of assaults upon himself.
> A: Yes; that is the object of it.[18]

Le Cras later tried to get the *Vingtenier* Mahy disciplined for failing to perform his duty; but he did not succeed. This, in his opinion, was another instance of the police protecting Seward, a viewpoint with which, as we shall see, the newspaper *Le Constitutionnel* fully agreed.

V

Two aspects of Le Cras' story are worth remarking upon. The first is that he was assaulted by a disgruntled reader; the second is that he started as, and continued to be, a seller of patent medicines.

Assault of newspaper editors was, if not frequent, at least commonplace in Jersey, although they sometimes gave as good as they got. It was an old tradition, in fact as old as the press itself on the island. Philippe Dumaresq, said to have introduced the printing press to Jersey in the second half of the 18th century, edited the island's first newspaper, the *Gazette de Jersey*. One day a man called Thomas Lemprière called at his office to demand the name of the writer of an article that had appeared. When it was refused, he distributed a printed note calling Dumaresq a coward. 'Some days later,' according to *A Biographical Dictionary of Jersey*, 'they met in the Market Place, and "walking sticks came into play." Mr Lemprière began to retreat beneath the weight of the adversary's blows. Then a vigorous stroke on his arm caused him to drop his stick. Mr. Dumaresq immediately seized his opponent's ear with one hand, while with the other thrashed him soundly. During this correction Mr Lemprière tore Mr Dumaresq's shirt from top to bottom, and smothered it with his own blood. Mr Dumaresq then dropped his stick, and got in some heavy blows with his fists, and ended by gripping his antagonist by both ears, and rubbing his nose again and again in the mud. Mr Lemprière was helped to the house of Dr Lerrier to have his wounds dressed.'

The founder-editor of *L'Impartial* and from 1845, after he was bankrupt, of *La Chronique de Jersey*, was Francois Amice Romeril. His career had been a colourful one until he took to journalism. Born in St Helier in 1804, he spent the years 1825 – 1830 in Paris, where he was the part-owner of an exhibition of performing snakes. His journalistic rivals called him 'the menagerie man', and said that his snakes' venom had got into his pen. The *Biographical*

34

Dictionary reveals that he had the distinction of being beaten *twice* on the same day, when, 'in 1840, he was thrashed in the street twice in a single day by members of the Le Quesne family for a sarcastic article.'

Romeril brought a prosecution against the Le Quesnes, but was hoist on his own legal-technicality petard:

> Two months before he had wriggled out of a libel action brought by Dean Jeune by pleading that the Dean had sued Francois Romeril, whereas he was Francois Amice Romeril. His assailants now escaped by pleading that they were charged with assaulting Francois Romeril who, so the court had decided, did not exist.

Two years later, Romeril was in trouble again for 'tilting against the hospital administration.' The three sons of Edouard Sullivan, the Director of the Hospital, waylaid him, and, according to the *Chronique*, 'Jean Sullivan knocked him down with a blow of his fist, and then administered sound correction with a whip'; but, according to the *Miroir*, Romeril had the best of the tussle:

> 'When Sullivan stopped, Romeril made for him, armed with a life-preserver, a whalebone implement with a ball of lead at the end. His brother ran to his rescue, but received a blow on the head, which would have cracked a skull less thick than him but at the cost of a bruise and the loss of his hat he enabled the hero of the whip to escape.'

The tendency to be assaulted was passed on to his son, Charles. According to the *Constitutionnel* of 23 May, 1846, which rejoiced in the opportunity to attack the police:

The two sons of the *Centenier Chevalier* armed themselves with cudgels to revenge themselves upon Mr. Charles Romeril for a joke they attributed to him, and in dark shadow they, the children of Light, flung themselves on the inoffensive young man, threw him to the ground and, at the risk of killing him, or at least of injuring him for the rest of his life, heaped blows upon him!

In the florid style typical of that newspaper, the report continues:

Nota bene the generosity of this proceeding. They were two, two young men who, the better to overwhelm their victim, waited until dark to attain their end and violate the public peace. Oh, we will be told, perhaps, that they were not the police. That is true; but their father was, and one of them was added to the roll of the police after having given this proof of his *savoir faire*. Thus the guardians of the peace!

The 'joke' was an article that Charles Romeril had written back in 1845, whose inoffensiveness is an indication of how, in small and enclosed communities, passions can run high over the veriest trifles:

The police of St Helier, as everyone knows, is made up of young men, *bon vivants*, liking, among other things, pleasure and a good time. That is not forbidden. Now one day in July, 1845, these gentlemen, to have a break from their labours, clubbed together to go to the country and enjoy a picnic. There is nothing bad in that. No, not at all.

But unhappily a journalist had the misfortune to write that one brought wine to the party; another brandy; and the *Centenier* Chevalier tripe and black pudding. This one fact, the only detail to describe the food that the police did or did not enjoy that day, brought the sons of M. Chevalier to attack the indiscreet narrator...[1]

The editor of *Le Constitutionnel*, Jean Nicolas René De La Croix, who will feature importantly in subsequent pages, was also no stranger to being assaulted:

He was constantly in hot water. In 1838 he was horsewhipped in the street in the presence of his school-children for an article he had written. In 1840 he demanded an explanation from H. L. Manuel, who had called him a 'penny-a-liner', but retired with two black eyes and a bloody nose.[2]

Editing newspapers in Jersey, then, though a sedentary occupation, seemed not to be without its physical hazards, and Le Cras was clearly far from the only editor to suffer (or provoke) assault.

As we have seen, Le Cras started out as a patent medicine seller; and, though he rose to literature, never gave it up. Again, he was far from unique in this; there was a very close relationship between the provincial press and patent medicine in this era.

Of the seven Jersey newspapers mentioned in *The Newspaper Press Directory* of 1846, three were either owned or edited by patent medicine sellers, and this was, if anything, below the average for British provincial newspapers. In Whitehaven, for example, both the newspapers, the *Whitehaven Herald* and the *Cumberland Pacquet* were owned by such; the owners of all three Sheffield newspapers, the *Sheffield Independent*, the *Iris* and the *Sheffield Mercury*, were likewise vendors of patent medicines. Two of the three Shrewsbury newspapers, the *Shrewsbury Chronicle* and *Eddowe's Journal*, were owned by patent medicine sellers. And so on and so on.

The reason for this connection is obvious on looking into the newspapers: the largest single category of advertisement in them by far is that for patent medicines, and so there was a natural synergy between the two occupations, newspaper proprietor or editor, on the one hand, and patent medicine seller on the other. The newspaper owners were, in effect, paid and made a profit twice over: first on their advertising space, and then on the sale of the products advertised in their pages.[3]

About half of the advertisements for patent medicines were for alleged remedies for syphilis and other venereal diseases. To put it melodramatically, the prevalence of syphilis funded the press.

> THE CONCENTRATED DETERSIVE ESSENCE
> An anti-syphilitic remedy for searching out and purifying the diseased humours of the blood.
> Venereal contamination, if not at first eradicated, will often remain secretly lurking in the system for years, and although for a while undiscovered, at length will break out upon the unhappy individual in its most dreadful forms; or else unseen, internally endanger the very vital organs of existence.

In the case of syphilis, of course, this is no more than the truth; though whether the 'detersive essence' exercised the effect claimed may be rather doubted. Incidentally, the recognition that syphilitic infection could have effects many years later was surely an intellectual triumph, or a triumph at least of patient and careful observation.

In addition to the Detersive Essence was the *Cordial Balm of Syriacum*, successor in the market to Dr Solomon's *Cordial Balm of Gilead*[4]:

This medicine is particularly to be taken *before
persons enter into the* MATRIMONIAL STATE, lest
in the event of procreation occurring, the innocent
offspring should bear estamped upon it the physical
characteristics derivable from parental debility.

This advertisement, too, played upon a real and reasonable
fear; though it might be doubted whether Cordial Balm of
Syriacum should, with reason, have allayed it.

Perry's Purifying Essence did the same job, while The Silent
Friend (distributed by post in sealed brown envelopes, like bribes)
cured masturbation.

Another great problem was constipation, for which the
suggested solution was *Lord Eldon's Aperient Pills*. Lord Eldon, the
Lord Chief Justice and Lord Chancellor who lived to be 87, was
said by the advertisements that appeared in the Jersey newspapers
to have been a sufferer from this condition on account of his
sedentary occupations. His name could be taken in vain, for he
was dead; but the prestige attached to it evidently lived on.

The advertisement began with a ringing statement regarding
the origin of human disease, derived from the words of John
Abernethy, the eminent former surgeon to St Bartholomew's:

'Habitual costiveness,' said the late Mr Abernethy,
'I have no hesitation in saying, is the foundation or
forerunner of every disease to which the human
frame is subject.'

This would seem to mean that, but for constipation, man would
be immortal, a view with which my late grandmother would have
heartily concurred.

The medicine was advertised as having been tested and found
free of all mercurial substances, hitherto used as a laxative with
horrific side-effects, by no less a figure than Andrew Ure, MD,

FRS. Ure was a man of parts; the first consulting chemist, he was one of the founders of the popular scientific lecture, he is suspected of having been the model for Dr Frankenstein (in 1818, he applied a strong electric current to the body of an executed murderer, causing it to jerk in a life-like way), he was an apologist for the factory system of the 1830s, writing a book, *The Philosophy of Manufactures*, that was quoted by Marx and Engels, and he made important contributions to theoretical chemistry. Did he, then, really apply 'a careful chemical analysis' to *Lord Eldon's Aperient Pills*? I suspect that he did, for he was a fiery and litigious man, sometimes described as vain and pompous, who would not have suffered his name to be taken in vain.

But by far the single most regular and prolific advertiser in the Jersey newspapers was Thomas Holloway, who practically invented mass advertising. He had two products, his pills and his ointment, which he marketed more or less as a panacea. Week after week, he bombarded the public with testimonials to miracle cures such as the following:

> Statement under oath given before the Lord Mayor of London:
> William Brooke, messenger, lives at No. 2, Union Street, Southwark, swears and says that he had 15 suppurating ulcers and unhealed sores on his left arm and two legs. Because of this, he was received as an out-patient at the Metropolitan Hospital for nearly four weeks. As he had no relief, he gave up hope of being cured there and went to the three following hospitals: King's College for five weeks; Guy's Hospital for six; and Charing Cross for several. He left the last worse than when he left Guy's Hospital, after Mr Bransby Cooper, like the other doctors there, told him 'the only way of saving your life is amputation of your arm.'

He then went to Dr Bright, chief physician to Guy's Hospital, who, after seeing his condition, said ashamed, 'I can do absolutely nothing to cure you, but here is half a sovereign; go to Mr Holloway and try his pills and his ointment; I have several times witnessed the marvellous effect that they have had in hopeless cases. Come back to see me afterwards.'
The result was dramatic: After three weeks his cure was complete. When Dr Bright saw the result of his charitable advice, he said, 'I am altogether gratified and astonished, because I thought that I should never see you again, unless without your arm. This cure is really marvellous.'

This is an audacious advertisement, because Dr Bright, the discoverer of Bright's disease (glomerulonephritis), was then at the height of his fame, being among the most celebrated physicians of Europe. And Bransby Cooper was by no means unknown either – we shall meet him again briefly later on. It required no slight courage for a patent-medicine manufacturer to quote two eminent medical men acknowledging their powerlessness by comparison with patent medicine, especially when one of them (Bransby Cooper) was known to be litigious. Perhaps, then, Cooper and Bright really did say the things alleged in the advertisement.

Holloway did not believe in half-measures when it came to making claims on his products' behalf:

> This extraordinary ointment cures the most dangerous sores and ulcers, weakness of the legs, diseases of the chest and throat, yaws, African leprosy, cancers, haemorrhoids, swellings, scrofulas, scurf, chilblains, gout, rheumatics and almost all the maladies of the skin – including mosquito and sandfly bites.

41

He also had another technique. Week after week, he caused reports of remarkable cures allegedly brought about by his pills and ointment all over the world to be inserted in the Jersey newspapers as if they were news rather than advertisement. Here, under the headline 'An obstruction of the liver cured by Holloway's Pills,' is one that occurred locally to his centre of operations, London:

> Mrs Mary Sandford, Leather Lane, Holborn, suffered an illness of the liver for five years, which caused indigestion, and intermittent migrainous blindness; she was depressed and very irritable; she was sleepy and her stomach and legs swelled; she became very weak. She stayed three years in a hospital; but she had gone from bad to worse and had no hope of cure, when, having used these pills for only two months, she recovered perfect health.

One notes that she did not recover her health until she had taken her pills for two months; obviously, Holloway wanted his pills to work miracle cures, but not too quickly. Other testimonials came from as far away as Tobago and Van Diemen's Land.

Holloway made an immense fortune, though as much from investing his profits wisely as from the original profits themselves. He was a philanthropist: he founded the Royal Holloway College, spending the modern equivalent of £70 million to found and endow it.

Truly, as Hegel said, the owl of Minerva takes light at dusk.

VI

Having sent 11 *filles publiques* from Madame Le Gendre's *maison de débauche* to the General Hospital, M. *le Centenier* Le Cronier (whose son John and grandson Maxwell were doctors, the former a founding member of the *Société Jersiaise*, the latter the first president of the Jersey Wanderers Football Club, a post he held for a quarter of a century) returned to Mulberry Cottage.

Was Le Cronier following normal procedure in sending the young women to the General Hospital? The surviving hospital records of that time are very sparse, one of the only documents I managed to find being the hospital admission book for 1849. All this contains is the name of the patients received, their age, and the reason for, and date of, their admission. They are written in French.

The General Hospital was clearly very general, being an institution of diffuse purpose. One man was received there for murder, and two for crime. Only a relatively few were received for illness in general, frenzy, venereal disease, blindness, *aliénation mentale* and epilepsy being other (and rare) categories. The overwhelming majority of the 2,025 patients received that year, if that is what they should be called, were suffering from intemperance or destitution. However, there were 63 admissions for prostitution, involving 50 women, 13 of whom were admitted twice.

Most of the admissions were for women acting singly, but there were two occasions when a brothel seems to have been cleared out when eight women were admitted on the same day, one of whom on each occasion was conspicuously older than the rest, being 48 and 47 years, and who may therefore be presumed to have been the *madame* of the enterprise. The youngest woman admitted for prostitution was 17.

The women taken on those occasions might be presumed to be professional, as perhaps were those single operators who were admitted twice. But prostitution was clearly a seasonal business in Jersey, for almost all the admissions were in the summer months. There is more than one possible explanation of this seasonality, of course. It is possible that some women (local or foreign) took the opportunity to earn a little extra money provided by the increasing number of English visitors to the island, it having become a tourist destination in that decade. It is possible that, the weather being clement, the prostitutes were more inclined to solicit in the streets than at other times of the year, thus making themselves more visible to the police. It is possible that the police themselves were more active in the summer months, preferring to stay indoors when it was cold. What one can say is that the admission of prostitutes to the General Hospital was as seasonal (at least in 1849) as the potato harvest.

Prostitution was evidently quite widespread in St Helier in the mid-19th century, perhaps not surprisingly because, according to Victor Hugo[1], who was exiled from France to Jersey for four years before moving to Guernsey, St Helier was the seventh largest port town or city of Great Britain, and it also had quite a large garrison of soldiers. Fort Regent was built during the Napoleonic Wars as a bulwark against possible French invasion, and designed for 31 officers and 448 non-commissioned officers and privates, though in its time it had housed up to 1,468 soldiers.[2] The men were without their families, if indeed they had one; it was not surprising, then, that there were streetwalkers in St Helier.

The records do not state whether the *filles publiques*, once in hospital, underwent medical examination for venereal disease; nor what work they were put to once held there, or for how long. They could not have been held for very long, however, for by the latter half of the season the proportion of them admitted for a second time in the year went up dramatically. Among their number was one called Ann Le Noble, aged 25. She could not have been the daughter of Marie Le Noble (or Le Gendre), owner of the Mulberry Cottage brothel; the census of 1841 does not record an Ann Le Noble living with Marie Le Noble at that time. It is probable, however, that she was a cousin. And it is likely that several pairs of sisters were involved in the trade; for example, Esther and Ellen Syvret, 22 and 27 years old respectively. Ann de Jersey, aged 19 and one of the women admitted twice to the hospital, was recorded as having been born in the hospital, a sign that she was illegitimate and quite possibly the daughter herself of a prostitute. Her surname was suggestive of her lack of parentage, although the family name of de Jersey does exist.

It is unlikely that the police removed all the prostitutes of the town into the hospital. Why these, then? A scandal occurring later in the century, known as 'the Paid Police Scandal', might explain why Elizabeth Garland and Jane Brown, the two presumptive brothel-keepers, were selected. The police were accused in 1895 both of procuring for the brothel-keepers and of running a protection racket. In his *Brothels and Houses of Ill-fame in Jersey 1790 – 1918*, Nicholas Le Cornu relates details of the trial. 'A Mrs Brett, when asked if she kept a house of ill-fame in Hilary Street, replied "she had a kind of lodging house (laughter in the Court)… she gave [the Police] money because they showed gentlemen to her house and brought friends to the door."'

A Miss Denman, a prostitute living in Miss Brett's house, told the court that two policemen, Huggins and McFarling, had brought a gentleman to the house, and afterwards requested money from her for providing the customer. She gave them a shilling each, they called back the following day, unsatisfied, and unsuccessfully demanded more from Mrs Brett.[1]

The brothels, such as that at Mulberry Cottage, probably catered to a different class of client from that of the single streetwalker, though the personnel overlapped. Two of the women taken in the round-ups at brothels were also taken singly at other times; while four of the women, presumably more professional, were removed from both brothels. Madame Le Gendre probably catered for the upper or courtesan end of the market, for it was

45

noted at the time, not without a certain *frisson* of outrage, that Mulberry Cottage 'had iron gates and a 12-foot wall topped with broken bottles, obscuring the view of passers-by. The windows had shutters that excluded all light and inside was a well-furnished ballroom with rugs, sofas, three gold clocks and a timepiece.'[4]

These effects were subsequently sold at auction, in the presence of a legal officer, and 'the crowd that had rushed to see the *maison de débauche* after the crime rushed likewise to the sale.'[5]

The 1830s, that is to say the end of the pre-Victorian era, were the high point of police action against brothels on Jersey. In that decade there were nine prosecutions for keeping them; in every other decade until the turn of the century (when the population was larger), there were only four per decade on average.[6]

In the 1870s there existed in Jersey the equivalent of the lap-dancing club, though somewhat more forthright. In 1871 there was a house in Charles Street, run by Charles Laray and wife in which 'four French prostitutes were being forced to perform before groups of six to 20 men, who paid to enter and drink champagne, and watch naked scenes of "which modesty does not permit description."'

It was to be part of Madame Le Gendre's defence that she was not the only one to run a *maison de débauche*, with the implication that it was unfair or unjust that she should have been singled out.

VII

On the day, Thursday, before he was fatally wounded, Le Cronier returned to Mulberry Cottage with four of the women he had caused to be admitted to the hospital and who needed their clothes that were still at the cottage. Madame Le Gendre refused to hand them over, claiming that they belonged to her. According to the *Chronique de Jersey*, Émile Cousin visited Madame Le Gendre that same evening. Mme Le Gendre was clearly furious at the actions of Le Cronier. 'I am buggered,'[1] she apparently, said, 'if I don't take the knife and rip his guts.'

'She appeared angry,' said Cousin, 'but completely sane. She was seated in a chair next to the fire and said this to me quietly. Her husband Pierre Le Gendre was also in the room, and hearing her say this, he said "*Oh! bah, bah, ma fille, tu ne voudrais pas le faire.*"'[2]

The next day, Friday, the junior police officer, Henry-Luce Manuel, went to Le Cronier's home, where he found him writing a report about someone called Eva at whose house there had been some kind of uproar the previous Sunday. Le Cronier was writing the names of four '*filles*' who had been seized at Eva's house (more prostitutes, perhaps) when he suddenly said to Manuel, 'Oh, I have orders to seize Madame Le Gendre, to bring her to court tomorrow,' and he asked Manuel to accompany him to Mulberry Cottage.

Apparently the authorities had received a letter of complaint from neighbours about the constant disorders at that address, and deemed it time to act. Le Cronier and Manuel set out.

As luck, or perhaps premeditation, would have it, Madame Le Gendre had a large carving knife professionally sharpened the very morning of Le Cronier's next appearance at Mulberry Cottage.

She had been talking in her house to her neighbour, M. Philippe De Gruchy, when Le Cronier appeared on the horizon with Manuel. De Gruchy came to ask Madame Le Gendre for repayment of a small debt, but she said that she could not pay because Le Cronier had deprived her of her living. The police had seized her girls, she said; she was surprised that they were so severe with her when there were so many other such houses kept by foreigners that were much more disorderly than hers, and she being a native of the country. She said that if the authorities would not give her justice, she would take it for herself. De Gruchy told her to pipe down or she would get into trouble; she maintained that she had said no more to him than she had said to Le Cronier himself. De Gruchy then left, Madame Le Gendre following him, outdoors reiterating how Le Cronier had seized her girls. It was then that she saw Le Cronier approach, whereupon she exclaimed, '*Voici venir le vieux batarde.*'[3] ('Here comes the old bastard.')

According to Manuel, both he and Le Cronier had gone to Mulberry Cottage completely unarmed, without even their truncheons, because they anticipated no resistance from Madame Le Gendre. When she saw them, she ran into the cottage, going into a parlour on the left. She had time, it appears, to warn the two young women who had come to lodge with her three days before, presumably as partial replacements for the 11 young women removed to hospital the previous Sunday[4], to hide upstairs.

Mr Le Cronier said a few words to Mr De Gruchy, and then followed Madame Le Gendre into the parlour. She stood by a table between two windows overlooking the garden. She asked Mr Le Cronier what he wanted; he replied that he had orders that she should appear before the court tomorrow. Madame Le Gendre replied, 'Of course, you know perfectly well, M. Le Cronier, that I can justify myself.' He said, 'And you know perfectly well that it is not to me that you have to justify yourself, but to the court.' Then he added that she had to furnish bail to appear in court the following day at 11 o'clock.

Madame Le Gendre said, 'My husband is not here, so I cannot give you bail.' 'In that case,' replied Le Cronier, 'you will have to come with me to prison.' She refused three times, saying 'I'm not going.' Then, 'calmly', she half-turned to the table and sprang towards Le Cronier, plunging a knife (the one she had had sharpened, that she had presumably placed on the table earlier) into his stomach. Here I may add that Madame Le Gendre was a professional, not an amateur: she struck upwards, which is dangerous, not downwards, which is theatrical. In doing so, she uttered a single, highly expressive syllable: *La!*

Whether she said anything else it is not possible now to determine, although in the Bodleian Library's copy of *An Account of the Island of Jersey* by W. Plees ('Many years resident in that island'), published in 1817, there are, unaccountably, a miscellany of newspaper cuttings, including from the English press of the mid-19th century, one of which claims that Madame Le Gendre said, on stabbing Le Cronier, 'Take that, you _____[5], that's my security!'

Le Cronier let out a loud cry; and in the same instant, Madame Le Gendre hurled herself at Henry-Luce Manuel, as if she would stab him too. He ran out, pursued by her with the knife still in her hand and covered in blood. He shouted 'Murder!' and signalled to the people in the street to come to his assistance. Instead, they went into a shop; Mr Manuel later followed in their direction and said 'For God's sake, come and help me, Mr Le Cronier has been murdered!'[6]

Mr Le Cronier had run out into the street, where Mr Manuel joined him. Mr Le Cronier said, *'Oh, mon garçon, je suis stabbé!'*

Madame Le Gendre approached them, knife still in hand; but then she suddenly turned away towards a wall, over which she flung the knife. Mr Manuel asked the people who had come back out into the street to try to arrest the woman: he had now to attend to Mr Le Cronier. (Perhaps this was the wrong way round: he should have tried to arrest Madame Le Gendre, while they attended to Mr Le Cronier. But it was all in the heat of the moment.) When he reached Mr Le Cronier, the latter threw himself into his arms.

49

The fate of the knife in those days before there was much in the way of forensic testing was as follows: William Woodberry, aged 35, happened to be passing by with his cart at the material time when he saw M. Manuel leave the cottage and heard him shout 'Murder!' Then came M. Le Cronier, followed by Madame Le Gendre with a knife in her hand. Woodberry saw that Le Cronier had blood on his hands, at first thinking that Madame Le Gendre had merely stabbed his hands. He saw her throw the knife over the wall, and went to pick it up. As a crowd gathered to observe, or to gawp, and the news of the murderous attack spread, he gave the knife to a man called William-Visconte Le Quesne, aged 31, telling him that it was the knife that Madame Le Gendre had used. Le Quesne said that he could see no one in authority to take care of the knife, so he thought it was his duty to do so. Presumably Le Quesne was of higher social class than Woodberry, an employee of a coal-merchant, and in a hierarchical society being of higher social class was authority in itself. Le Quesne then gave the knife to the first police officer whom he found, M. Thomas Bichard. Bichard made a notch on its handle, to give it a distinguishing mark. It was later produced at the trial, where several people recognised it.

VIII

The way in which M. *le Centenier* Le Cronier met his death was
dignified, noble and moving. 'I have sent for you that you may
see how a Christian may die,' Addison is said to have told his
nephew on his deathbed; Le Cronier made no such boast, but still
he showed how a man might die.

When Le Cronier was in Manuel's arms, he said that he was a
dead man. Manuel replied, 'Don't be afraid, perhaps it's nothing
more than a pinprick. We'll laugh about it later.' Le Cronier
repeated that he was sure that he was mortally wounded. When
a M. Le Rossignol *fils* had joined them to lend his assistance, Le
Cronier said, 'Listen, *mes garçons*, I am a dead man; here is my last
wish: I give a third of all that I have to give to my wife.'

Mr Manuel said to him, 'Please, M. Le Cronier, do not talk
in that way.' But M. Le Cronier knew that he would die, and
repeated his last wish, adding: 'She has been a good wife – she will
take care of my children.'[1] The sincerity of these simple words is
obvious, one might almost say luminous.

Manuel and Le Cronier started to walk to the latter's home:
it did not occur to them to go to the hospital, which in those
days was more for the indigent and the vice-ridden than for the
wounded. On reaching the house of M. Bichard, in Sand Street,
Manuel suggested that Le Cronier rest there, but he did not want
to. A little further on, however, Manuel persuaded him to enter
the house of M. Binet, using the argument that if he arrived home
in his current state he would alarm his wife. Once in M. Binet's
house he lay down on a sofa and awaited medical attention.

Four medical men in total came to his aid, Drs Jones, Fixott,
Quesnel and Dickson.[2] They could do little for him. When they
arrived, they found him very weak. In his evidence at the trial,
Dr Jones said that he was convinced from the moment that
he saw the wound that it was mortal; he sent for Advocate

Godfray so that Le Cronier could make a deathbed statement (a special legal weight attaching to the words and evidence of a dying man).

Dr Fixott in his evidence said that he had found M. Le Cronier pale and his pulse weak and irregular. He ordered a little wine for him, fearing that he would otherwise faint, and suggested that the patient remain calm while he examined him. He lifted the underclothes, all stained with blood, covering M. Le Cronier's abdomen and found an oblique stab-wound about two inches long, an inch and a half below and to the right of the umbilicus. Three inches of omentum (the folded part of the lining of the abdomen) had emerged through the wound. Not wanting to replace it by himself, he awaited the arrival of Dr Quesnel, Le Cronier's regular doctor, and together they put it back inside the abdominal cavity, then applying two sutures to close the wound and dressed it 'according to surgical principles' – which at the time, of course, did not include antisepsis, let alone asepsis.

M. Le Cronier asked Dr Fixott whether he was in danger; Dr Fixott said, 'Yes.' He then looked for other injuries, but found none in the abdomen, instead finding the classic sign of someone defending himself against a knife attack, a wound on the hand.

Believed, and believing himself, to be dying, Le Cronier dictated his will and signed it. This document is still to be found in the Jersey Archive.[3] To hold a document signed by a man who knows himself to have been murdered is a moving experience, and in some fashion brings home to the imagination the heinousness of the offence: and one can see his strength ebbing away in his signature, which starts more strongly than it finishes. A simple document, written in French, the will is stained by smears, one of which at least looks very like a bloodstain. Having signed his will, Le Cronier then made a solemn statement 'in the presence of death.'[4] He gave an account of the facts of the case, calmly and without exaggeration or rancour. It was read back to him and he signed it.

It was decided that M. Le Cronier should be returned to his home, and this was done. Dr Quesnel stayed with him as he grew ever-weaker until his death at 12.30 the following afternoon, which 'put an end to his suffering.' There is no record of him having uttered a word of complaint, though he suffered much pain and had vomited blood. His dignity was absolute.

A post mortem was carried out by the four doctors the next day. They found a wound not only in the omentum, but in the large bowel. There were two and a half pints of blood in the abdominal cavity. They came to the unsurprising conclusion that he died of wounds inflicted by a knife or a sword.

The day following his death, a Monday, the shops did not open as a mark of respect. The next issue of the *Chronique de Jersey*, on Wednesday, but not *Le Constitutionnel* the following Saturday, had heavy black lines of mourning running between the four columns of its pages.

IX

The killing of George Le Cronier, coming so soon after two others, caused genuine shock on the island. No policeman had ever been murdered before on Jersey, and none has ever been murdered since. Indeed, only one other has ever lost his life in the course of duty; Sergeant Frank John Dutot was killed on 28 April, 1949, when a racing car crashed into him while he was engaged on crowd control at the race.[1] Jersey is not the kind of place where it is dangerous to be a policeman.

On the day of the obsequies, all shops shut and the crowd going to the cemetery was so large that Le Cronier had been buried by the time the end of the procession reached it.[2] Somewhat absurdly in the circumstances, the *Chronique de Jersey* reported that Le Cronier had been a man 'who had no enemies.' Perhaps 'many enemies' would have been more apposite.

What kind of man was Le Cronier? It is not easy to say from the record. There is one engraved portrait of him, done after his death and sold in large numbers[3], by a Jersey artist called Thomas Berteau (1819 – 1904) who in his youth went to study in Paris and 'was tempted to assume French nationality so that he could compete in the Prix de Rome, but his father, a British sea-captain, would not have it.'[4]

A man called Robin Cox, who spent his life accumulating historical information of all kinds about Jersey, said that Le Cronier was not an attractive figure.[5] It is possible that corroborative evidence for this judgment exists somewhere in the 60 or more boxes of assorted papers that he left after his untimely death that are now lodged in the Jersey Archive, but the papers have yet to be classified and I have not been able to examine them. There are contemporary diaries also that I have not been able to read, that may contain references to him, laudatory or derogatory as the case may be. Certainly from Berteau's excellent portrait, which has the air of verisimilitude, and seems to be as concerned to convey character as surface likeness, Le Cronier was a severe and possibly a humourless man, though an upright one, even to the point of fanaticism. (The facsimile signature underneath the engraving is, not surprisingly, very much firmer than that appended to his will, though recognisably that of the same man.) I do not think one would lightly cheek George Le Cronier, or crack a joke with him. He looks like someone who has seen too much of the dark side of life for him to regard human existence as anything other than a very serious business, indeed something of a grind to be got through as best one can rather than a pleasure; but as his position was an honorary and elective one, it might be that he brought his temperament to his experience rather than his experience to his temperament. Furthermore, physiognomy, though we all practice it in an amateur fashion, is not an exact science; appearances, though we often have little else to go by, can be deceptive; and perhaps Le Cronier's Old Testament-prophet face relaxed into tenderness in the bosom of his family. Probably we will never know. According to the diaries of Colonel Sir John Le Couteur, Sheriff of Jersey and former aide-de-camp to both William IV and Queen Victoria, his two sons, who returned for the funeral from France where they were studying, did not appear much moved by their father's death: though whether this was indifference or self-control the diary does not say.

Almost immediately after Le Cronier's death, however, a collection was started towards erecting a monument to the memory of the murdered policeman. Within a week, more than £300 had been collected, a very considerable sum, the equivalent in purchasing power today of perhaps £30,000.[6] This might not have been a simple testimony to Le Cronier's personal popularity, however, but rather an expression of outrage at the threat to law and order that his murder represented. At any rate, it took three years for the monument to be erected, such matters as its design and who should erect it causing a great deal of controversy. Near its completion, a construction worker called Bertaut fell from the top of the monument and was tended by Dr John Le Cronier, George Le Cronier's medical son. He was not seriously injured. Everyone was agreed that the monument was extremely tasteful, which indeed it is.

There is one other source of information on Le Cronier's character that I have found, in a curious book published in Jersey in 1847, *La Lyre Exilée (The Exiled Lyre)*, by a man called L. D. Hurel. The book was advertised for subscription in the *Chronique de Jersey* for 6 January, 1847, at '2 chelins [shillings] British' for residents of Jersey and Guernsey, and '3 chelins British' for residents of France and England, to be printed as soon as the quantity of subscriptions defrayed the costs of printing it. As far as I have been able to find, Hurel left no other trace of his earthly existence but this book[7], apart from one other in the Bibliotheque Nationale in Paris, entitled *Le petit Momus*.[8] Leonord Dumesnil Hurel seems to have been a French political refugee on the island during the reign of Louis Philippe, which suggests that he was a much more intransigent republican than the infinitely better-known French refugee, Victor Hugo, who arrived on the island five years later, in the wake of the coup of Louis Napoleon. The book is subtitled *Elegies, Varied Poems, Vaudeville Comedy and Songs*, among the latter of which is the *Chant funebre sur la mort de M. George Le Cronier*. This comes with an explanatory essay on the characters of Le Cronier and Le Gendre respectively.

According to this essay, the *Chant funebre* was printed separately after Le Cronier's death, in two editions of 2,000 copies each, which sold out, but did not exhaust the public demand in Jersey for his poem. If true (and I have no reason to suppose that it is not), it means that, at the very least, public feeling after Le Cronier's death was high; for, supposing an adult population of 25,000, of whom 20,000, four-fifths, were fully literate, with two such adults per household, L. D. Hurel's poem was bought by four of every 10 literate households, a penetration undreamed of by any author, let alone poet, today. And I have estimated conservatively.

Hurel's depiction of Le Cronier was unidimensional, as perhaps one would expect in the circumstances:

> M. George Le Cronier belonged to one of the most honourable and most honoured families of the island. He was a good husband, father and citizen. Sincerely attached to his country, he devoted 30 years to its service, and to defending it against the open and often concealed attacks of the enemies of its privileges and prosperity. His patriotism was always pure and disinterested. For nearly nine years he filled the *unpaid* position of *Centenier*, and, despite all the irritations and inconveniences of this job, neither the zeal nor the patriotism of *le Centenier* Le Cronier declined for an instant. In the exercise of his difficult and often painful duties, M. Le Cronier always showed himself humane and conciliatory. His prudence, his kindness and his extreme goodness could and should serve as models for all those who fill public positions. Thanks to his paternal advice, and to his affability, young people misled by the ardour of passions and by bad example not only did not have their reputations blackened by an appearance in court, but also, and above all, were returned to the good. There was no hatred, inveterate as it might be, that he did not know how to appease. He knew how to make himself liked and respected by all, because he was good and just towards all. But if he was indulgent towards the follies of youth, towards minor misdeeds, he was – we say it in praise of him – he was pitiless towards crime; he pursued it everywhere and always, without regard to wealth or rank. He was never one of those with two weights and two scales, and in this he was once again worthy

of serving as a model. It was, as we have pleasure in repeating, because he was just towards all, rich or poor, native or foreigner, that he was loved, respected, regretted and mourned by all, even his political opponents. The entire population came to attend his funeral. As soon as it was known that he was no more, all the shops shut as one, and all the flags in the port were flown at half-mast as a sign of mourning. The streets were deserted; each house seemed to be widowed.[9] The town was as gloomy and silent as the grave! Everyone seemed to have been stricken at once! Never had the memory of a man, a citizen of Jersey, not even of the highest or most important rank, no, not even a Governor, been accompanied to the field of rest by so innumerable and solemn a multitude. In this unparalleled crowd were spontaneously united all ranks of society, all political tendencies! all ages! There were not only compatriots, but English, French, Italians, Jews, Polish, Spanish, without distinction of religion or sect. And tears fell from every eye because they could not be held back! On all faces, sadly bowed, could be read the truest and profoundest pain! The cortege alone was made up of a thousand persons, all with black crepe round the hat and arms, and religiously followed by a crowd of people of both sexes. M. Le Cronier was not only a devoted citizen, a zealous public servant, intelligent, upright, a soft and affectionate husband, a loving and tender father, a man of irreproachable morals, he was also a generous and beneficent man, a philanthrope who, without ostentation, went secretly of his own accord to help the necessitous when the winter was hard and work was lacking. He was also a faithful,

true and useful friend, and if someone whom he
accounted friend (a name always sacred to him)
fell into hardship, he did not limit himself to sterile
consolatory words, or to superfluous good wishes,
but he did more, from his own purse and expense,
and – by an exquisite sense of delicacy of which
only noble souls are capable – he knew how to
spare the unfortunate friend the always humiliating
request for assistance, that is to say he gave it before
the person even dreamed of asking for it. No one
does not know that the unfortunate George Le
Cronier was the father of numerous family, sparing
no expense to assure the future of his children and
giving them a distinguished education, but that this
did not prevent him from being the protector of
and provider for six orphans, who found in him the
best of fathers.

Even allowing for the principle that one should say nothing but
good of the dead, or at least of the recently dead, this is fulsome,
and surely must have contained a large measure of truth, for if
it had been too far removed from reality it would have caused
hilarity. Hurel remarks upon the fact that 'as the victim of the
most cowardly murder, not a word of complaint or of vengeance
left his mouth against the wretch that struck him,' a fact that for
him showed 'what M. G. Le Cronier was.' As indeed it does.

It is perhaps not surprising, then, that Marie anne Le Gendre is
depicted in markedly less favourable terms:

> We had thought of retracing the life of the woman *Le
> Gendre*, but this life is so full of infamy and turpitude,
> the picture is in itself so disgusting, so ignoble, that
> our courage failed, and we shall say only that *Marie
> Le Noble* was born in the parish of Grouville in Jersey,

on 10 October, 1808, and that in 1829 she married a man by the name of *Pierre Marie Le Gendre*. Since her marriage, the woman *Le Gendre* has appeared several times before the Royal Court, under accusation of handling stolen goods and other misdeeds. This well-assorted couple kept a house of prostitution under the name, so disastrously well-known, of Mulberry Cottage. The woman *Le Gendre* had the most irascible, the most violent, the most vindictive and the most profoundly ferocious character that it is possible to imagine. In her, there was both tiger and hyena! And it was this woman, if one is permitted to give so sweet a name to such a monster, this impure woman, a thousand times more contemptible than the unfortunate prostitutes who inhabited her lair and whose debauchery she exploited, who deprived Jersey of one of its most honourable and useful citizens! Such was the loathsome woman who, in murdering a public servant in the exercise of his legal duty, plunged the whole population into mourning, and the most honourable family into eternal pain! Such was the fury who, by her crime, has destroyed all consolation, all joy, in the heart of a tender and chaste wife.

This all seems rather high-flown, perhaps, for present taste, but who is right, we or the Victorians? I am reminded of what the late John Gross wrote in the introduction to his marvellous *New Oxford Book of English Prose*:

> We should be… on guard, however, against a provincialism which estranges us from some of the great achievements of the past. If we don't distinguish between true eloquence and fake eloquence, if we

allow fear of pretentious or precious 'fine writing'
to frighten us off the real thing, the loss will be ours;
and it will be a large one.

Perhaps our fear of appearing ridiculous inhibits us from
entering imaginatively into Madame Le Cronier's mind after the
murder of her husband.

However, it must be admitted that Hurel's verses on the death of
Le Cronier are not the stuff of which literary immortality is made.
Just as someone once came away from a meeting with Mussolini
exclaiming 'Too many spats! Too many spats!' so one comes away
from Hurel's verses exclaiming, 'Too many exclamation marks!
Too many exclamation marks!' A sample will do:

> Il meurt assassiné!… Devant ce crime affreux,
> D'épouvante et d'effroi, monstre impie! odieux!
> Tu n'as pas reculé…. Jour a jamais funeste!
> Jour de deuil éternel!… vers la voute céleste
> Que de tristes regards se levent éperdus!
> Pleurez! peuple! pleurez! GEORGE CRONIER
> n'est plus!
> Or (Madame Le Cronier now lamenting):
> 'Il expire! il n'est plus!! Epouse infortunée!
> 'Il vaudrait mieux pour moi ne jamais etre née.
> 'Sur cette terre, hélas! qu'ai je a faire a présent?
> 'Dieux cruels! reprenez votre fatal présent!
> 'Tu n'es plus! cher époux! que m'importe la vie!
> 'Tu n'es plus! mon bonheur est a jamais détruit…' [10]

At 1.75 exclamation marks per line, this almost equals Coleridge
at his most emotionally dishonest, which is saying something.

If Hurel's contrast between the good Le Cronier and the evil
Le Gendre seems to us naïve or unrealistic in its starkness – we who
delight to dissolve all boundaries whatsoever, so that everything

may be permitted us with a clear conscience – he was at least cool and shrewd enough in his assessment of some of Madame Le Gendre's conduct after her arrest. He considers Madame Le Gendre's reading of the Bible in prison and her tendency to faint during her first appearances in court:

> The woman Le Gendre, whom we saw *piously* reading the Bible in her prison cell, in order to arouse interest and pity, fainted twice during her attendance in court on 24 March; her *weakness* was so great that the prison vehicle had to be employed to take her back to prison. On 26 March, her *extreme sensitivity* was such that she was unable to listen to the depositions of the witnesses, revealing the atrocious circumstances of the murder, and she once again fell into a *weakness!* She was sat down in an *armchair*, and two doctors, Messieurs G. Jones and Dickson, attended to her; despite this, she *fainted two or three more times*. The poor woman! Seeing that she lacked air, it was even necessary to remove her *hat and her boa, and open the doors and windows of the room!* Never were young misses surrounded by more delicate attentions than the worthy *mother* of Mulberry Cottage. And there were people naïve enough to believe in the reality of the nervous expressions of this monster!

Hurel's italicisation lets the reader know clearly enough what he thinks of Madame Le Gendre's character, shallow and attention-seeking. Certainly she seems to fit into the category of histrionic personality disorder, in which (according to the *Diagnostic and Statistical Manual of the American Psychiatric Association*) a person who has it shows 'a persistent pattern of excessive emotionality and attention-seeking, beginning by early adulthood and present in a variety of contexts, as indicated by five (or more) of the following:

1.is uncomfortable in situations in which he or she is not the center of attention of excessive emotionality and attention seeking, beginning by early adulthood

2.interaction with others is often characterized by inappropriate sexually seductive or provocative behavior

3.displays rapidly shifting and shallow expression of emotions

4.consistently uses physical appearance to draw attention to self

5.has a style of speech that is excessively impressionistic and lacking in detail

6.shows self-dramatization, theatricality, and exaggerated expression of emotion

7.is suggestible, i.e., easily influenced by others or circumstances

8.considers relationships to be more intimate than they actually are.'

Whether such a diagnosis genuinely furthers our understanding, or is merely a re-description or summary of observed behaviour, may well be doubted. It depends upon pattern-recognition: but whether the pattern recognised corresponds to a genuine condition or entity, which has definite causative antecedents, or is a mere cognitive artefact, is as yet unknown. At best, such pattern-recognition is a precondition of understanding; it does not constitute understanding in itself.

Another question is whether a person *has* or *is* a personality disorder. There are problems with both usages.

X

Madame Le Gendre's response to events was, also not surprisingly, different from that of the public at large. Having stabbed M. Le Cronier, she ran out of the house, disposed of the knife, and then ran back in, first having picked up a large stone and declared, in English, 'If any other gentlemen come here, I will be their butcher.' She was also heard to say, 'I've done for the bugger,' and, 'He would not give me satisfaction, but I've given the bastard satisfaction all right. I'm mad.'

She then ran briefly into the house of her neighbour, M. Letto, which, perhaps not coincidentally, appears to have been a tavern, but Mrs Letto said to her, 'For God's sake leave, I don't want anything to do with your affairs.' Uncharacteristically meek, Madame Le Gendre said, 'Yes, I'm going,' and M. Letto led her by the arm to the door.

Having returned to the house, she said to the two girls who had hidden upstairs during these events, 'I've stuck Le Cronier; I don't care, I have had my spite out of the Bugger.'[1] She then told the girls that they had nothing to fear.

M. Thomas Bichard, the police officer to whom Madame Le Gendre's knife was later entrusted, was the arresting officer. He went to Mulberry Cottage, where he found Le Gendre sitting on a chair in the parlour (even so banal a detail now seems infused with sinister meaning). Bichard said that she was his prisoner and that she must go with him. She said that she would not leave before having seen *le Centenier* Le Cronier, and that she was mad. Bichard took her by the arm and led her to the prison; she repeated several times on the way that she was mad.

One of the doctors who attended Le Cronier, Dr Jones, was also doctor to the prison. He went to see Madame Le Gendre in prison on the Sunday following the murder, in the company of MM. Bichard and *le Centenier* Chevalier. She said she was feeling much better and wanted the handcuffs removed, they having been placed on her an hour and a half earlier because she had said that she was mad and wanted to kill herself. Dr Jones did not order that they should be removed. The prisoner then volunteered that she had taken the knife, which was either on the table or the window sill, she could no longer remember which, and stabbed M. Le Cronier with it, saying that if she had to go to prison, it might as well be for a good reason.

On the following day, Monday, she repeated the story, this time in the presence of MM. Chevalier and Manuel, as well as Dr Jones, adding that, as a consequence of an article that she had read in the *Constitutionnel*, she believed that the police had no authority, and that they did not do their duty. This statement was to give rise to a lively, not to say acrimonious, controversy.

Dr Jones, evidently not feeling that he had sufficient authority, went to the President of the Prison Board, and told him why he believed he had had to apply handcuffs to Madame Le Gendre. The President went with him to the prison and ordered that Madame Le Gendre should be placed under surveillance by day, and handcuffed by night.

M. Chevalier deposed at the inquest into M. Le Cronier's death that, when he visited Madame Le Gendre in prison, he had found her sitting on her bed, reading the Bible. '*Malheureuse!*' he said to her. 'If you had always read books like that, you wouldn't be where you are.' [2]

She replied, 'No, that's right; but unfortunately I was reading something else.'

M. Chevalier then asked to know what could have induced her to commit such a murder, to which she replied that she considered M. Le Cronier as her enemy, and that, at the very moment the knife came back from the knife-grinder's, she had seen and read an article in *Le Constitutionnel* about a café-owner who had beaten a man called Le Cras, and according to the article, the police had done nothing so that it was time for people to take justice into their own hands. At this precise moment, she decided to murder the first member of the police who entered her house, above all M. Le Cronier.[3]

M. Chevalier also deposed the inquest that when he had searched Mulberry Cottage in the company of the *Connétable* of St Helier, M. Le Sueur, he had found two numbers of *Le Constitutionnel*, one that recounted the story of the assault on Mr Le Cras, and the other that carried the editor's claims that he was writing *'Le Livre Noir'* (*The Black Book*) of Jersey, in which he would reveal all the corruption of the island's élite.[4]

The legal process in Jersey was unique to itself, and quite unlike that of either England or France; it was derived from old French Norman customary law.

In a case such as that of the murder of Le Cronier, first came the inquest, called the *levée-de-corps*. This was held on Sunday, the day following Le Cronier's death, and the jury was like a coroner's jury in England. In this case it went first to the house of the deceased, then to Mulberry Cottage and finally to the hospital, where it heard the depositions. It came to an unsurprising verdict:

> That the said M. Le Cronier died on the afternoon of
> Saturday 28 February, 1846, as a result of a wound
> he received in the abdomen, on the afternoon of
> the preceding day, while in the course of fulfilling
> his duties as a Centenier; and that the said wound
> was caused by a deliberate and premeditated stab
> with a knife by Marie-Anne Le Noble, wife of
> Pierre Le Gendre.

Then came the trial-proper, known as *l'enditement*. This was held in front of three judges, one of whom was the Bailiff of Jersey, the highest-ranking official on the island, apart from the Lieutenant-Governor, whose position was more ceremonial than anything else. There was a jury of 13; normally it was a jury of honorary policemen of the parish in which the alleged crime was committed, but in this case, because of the crime's unusual nature, the jury was composed of policemen from other parishes. Needless to say, the *enditement* as a process was heavily criticised because the very corps of men whose duty it was to bring charges and gather evidence against someone were then asked to sit in judgment over him; in other words, they were asked to give a verdict on their own activities, and it was unlikely that they would find their own work deficient.

The force of this criticism was recognised in part in *l'enditement* of Madame Le Gendre. The Attorney-General, who prosecuted the case, opened by saying that he thought it appropriate to convoke a jury not from the police of St Helier, where the crime had been committed, to avoid all suspicion of collusion, hatred or partiality on the part of the jury. This was unusual, he said, but not unprecedented: and he cited the precedents.

All the evidence deemed relevant to the case was heard at the *enditement*.

Once an accused had been found guilty by the *enditement*, he or she could then appeal to *la Grande Enquête du pays*. This was composed of a jury of 24 householders of the parish, 20 of whom had to agree on a verdict for it to stick. If someone was charged with murder but five jurors thought him not guilty of the crime, he was acquitted of it; but the same jury could then find him guilty of a lesser crime, for example of culpable homicide instead of murder. In other words, the jury sought the highest common denominator.

The procedure of *la Grande Enquête du pays* was truncated, however; it did not hear all the evidence over again. Instead, it heard only the closing arguments of the defence and prosecution. Its verdict was final – except, as we have seen, for appeal to the Royal Prerogative, exercised in practice by the Home Secretary.

The *enditement* of Madame Le Gendre took place on Saturday, 18 April, 1846, exactly seven weeks after Le Cronier's death. Madame Le Gendre was defended by Advocate Hammond.[1] The evidence taken was very similar to that given at the *levée-du-corps*, not surprisingly because it was the same people giving it. In any case, the facts were hardly in dispute; the trial, rather, turned on the degree of Madame Le Gendre's culpability. Everything depended on the closing speeches, particularly on Mr Hammond's.

Hammond, it was reported, rose to speak amidst 'the most profound silence.' He didn't have a strong hand to play, of course, the facts being agreed and not looking very much in Madame Le Gendre's favour, so he sought to overwhelm the jury by the citing of precedents, by a certain amount of hair-splitting, by long-windedness that gave the impression that there was a great deal to say, and by subtly implying that the murder was partly the victim's own fault for exceeding his authority as a policeman. His time-honoured method was to try to throw dust in the jury's eyes; he adopted the wise maxim (wise in the circumstances, that is), that when you have little to say, say it lengthily and repeat it many times, for a repetition with slight variation often gives the impression of being a new argument. Here is what he said:

> *Monsieur le Bailli* [Bailiff], *Messieurs les Juges* [Judges], *Messieurs l'Enditement* [Jury], in coming before you as the defender of the unhappy woman in the dock, I must first observe that I do not intend to contest the principal facts of the case. I do not have to waste time on these facts because they have been so clearly proved by the prosecution that I have to admit that a most frightful crime has been committed – that the unhappy woman in the dock has hands stained with the blood of the late Centenier, M. Le Cronier; and rest assured, *Messieurs*, that when a spontaneous and general cry of pain went up in all parts of this island, my foolingn were thom of my fellow chluouru, of my country. No one regrets the late M. Le Cronier more than the defender of the prisoner; I knew him intimately, and I had several occasions on which to admire his goodness and humanity.
>
> I know that you are here today called upon to fulfil a duty, a duty that must be very painful for you; and I know that moral courage is about to be tested,

for I have to ask of you not a verdict of acquittal, but of a modification of the charge.

I now come to the matter in hand. The charge against the unhappy Marie-Anne Le Noble, the prisoner in the dock, is that of having caused the death of M. *le Centenier* Le Cronier while fulfilling the duties of his position. I will have to examine the facts; but before that, I believe it is necessary to explain to you what kind of homicide we have to consider; I will also have to explain the law to you, in order for you to know if, when M. Le Cronier entered the house of Pierre-Marie Le Gendre, he was authorised to do so. I dispute the legality of this act without this in any way reflecting upon the character of the late M. Le Cronier. If a public servant, in pursuance of his duty, illegally enters a house and is killed at that moment, the homicide is only *manslaughter*[2]; for when he acts under the rule of law he receives every protection; but when he acts illegally, and is repulsed by blows, and these blows have the most unfortunate consequences, they can only be considered as simple homicide or *manslaughter.*

Now, *Messieurs*, you will take clear note that Pierre-Marie Le Gendre, the husband of the prisoner in the dock, rented a house from M. Nicolas Le Bas, in Patriotic Place, some years ago; in 1844, he rented another house adjoining, from Jean Langlois, Esquire; and that, with the agreement of the owners, he had a communicating door made between these two houses. M. Marett has told you that he has considered this house as one of prostitution for about two years. M. Thomas Bichard likewise said that he had searched this house for girls, according to the orders of the *Connétable*. In other words, no complaint was brought to the court during the first five or six years that the first house was occupied, and no *Centenier* or police officer had to go there without a *Connétable*'s order to do so. This is very important because until the month of February this house was conducted just as before, without disturbances or disorders; and then the police went there to seize the prisoner who lived there.

Now, in what circumstances did they go? A disturbance took place the previous Saturday at the house of someone called Eva on the Parade; the domestic of Lieutenant-Colonel Mourant was dangerously wounded. M. *le Centenier* Le Cronier arrested the individuals who had started this fight and put them in prison; after which he went to Mulberry Cottage and removed eleven girls whom he then placed in the Hospital; that could hardly have been under any kind of suspicion of crime, for then he would have put them in prison.

Why did he not arrest Le Gendre at the same time, why did he not arrest him afterwards? Two or three days afterwards, M. Le Cronier returned to Mulberry Cottage and demanded to be given the clothes of the eleven girls he had previously lodged in the hospital. Why did he not arrest La Gendre, husband and wife, then? Until that moment, therefore, there was nothing legally against them. The following Friday, M. Le Cronier went once again to the house to arrest the woman Le Gendre, and it was clear that it was with the intention of arresting her alone because, according to the deposition of M. Manuel, they did not take their

71

truncheons with them, as surely they would have done if they had intended to arrest Pierre-Marie Le Gendre, he being a strong and robust man. When these two gentlemen caught sight of Madame Le Gendre she was speaking to M. De Gruchy at the door of her house; M. Le Cronier then entered a room in it and said to her that he had come to arrest her or get her to enter security to appear in court the next day.

She replied, 'My husband is not here, I have done nothing, and I cannot give any security.'

There is one other thing, *Messieurs*, that I have to say in addition to prove that it was well known that Pierre-Marie Le Gendre was the master of this house, and that is that he kept a vehicle with two horses, and that he paid the parish road tax; he kept this vehicle no doubt to increase the trade and to entice others to enter the house.

I base my argument, first that M. *le Centenier* Le Cronier had no right to arrest the prisoner without a written warrant, either of the Chief Magistrate or of the *Connétable*; and that, if he entered Mulberry Cottage without *warrant*[3] or order, he entered illegally and without authorisation: a fatal blow struck in such circumstances can only be considered simple homicide or *manslaughter*.

Second, if this house had been kept as a *maison de débauche*, there was no right of arrest without a court order, which could have been made with a view to bringing the keepers of the *maison* to court.

Third, I cannot accept the validity of the way of proceeding against Pierre-Marie Le Gendre and his wife because I maintain that they could not rightly be summarily arrested on the basis of a letter of complaint against them by their neighbours, but only by virtue of a report to the Court by the *Connétable* or the *Centeniers*.

And fourthly, in the event that *le Centenier* Le Cronier was acting within his rights to make an arrest, whether it be with or without the order of the Bailiff or the *Connétable*, he ought to have arrested Pierre-Marie Le Gendre, who kept the *maison de débauche*, for it was incorrect to act against the woman alone, but only as an accessory to her husband; and that if she had been presented in court, she would not have been allowed to reply to questions without her husband being present.

Now, as to the powers of the *Connétables*, they have not the right to make an arrest without a *warrant* or order, unless the persons be taken *in flagrante delicto*, which is clearly explained in Blackstone[4], page 292; but, giving all benefit of the doubt to the police, there had not been a breach of the public peace at the house known as Mulberry Cottage. I know that the *Connétables* have every right to search any house or place; I recognise their right to arrest any person caught *in flagrante*; but if it is alleged that a person keeps a *maison de débauche*, or that it is a public nuisance, the correct manner of proceeding is to present a report to the Court, and make the accused person appear before the Court.

Now I am going to show you that it is as a public nuisance that *maisons de débauche* are classified by Blackstone himself, for on page 166 he says that *bawdy houses*[5] are to be considered nuisances. I will refer you to a case in Jersey, very similar to the present one, in which proceedings were taken after a report to the Court; but at the same time,

I am not claiming that such establishments should be tolerated, or that it is not the duty of the police to suppress public nuisance or scandal. But until there is a breach of the public peace, summary arrest cannot be made without order of the court. In 1795, Amice Gallichan and Elizabeth Picot, his wife, were presented in court, by virtue of a report by M. *le Centenier* Aubin, of the parish of St Saviour, showing that they kept a disorderly house, and that she abused her husband; she was condemned to six weeks of imprisonment and ordered to give a security against her good conduct. In this case, she certainly kept a disorderly house, it was a public scandal, and she was brought to court by means of a report. In 1796, it was by means of a *Connétable*'s report that George-Hélier Hamon, accused of the rape of a 13-year-old girl, was brought to the bar; I know that the *Connétable* would have had the right to arrest him summarily, but I will cite other examples where this precedent was followed. In 1798, a certain Mackenzie, an innkeeper, who was accused of keeping his inn open after hours, was arrested by virtue of a Court order. On 15th September, 1798, the court ordered that Susanne Le Gros, found *in flagrante* keeping a *maison de débauche*, be arrested, the *Connétable* of St Mary having furnished a report against her.

I must here observe that there have been actions before the court against the irregularities and illegalities committed by some members of the police; and I know of one M. Salmon, who was relieved of his post, as a consequence. In 1789, one Jean Laurens was arrested by the *Centenier* Nicolle, of the parish of St Lawrence, for having maltreated his wife, and was put in gaol without the order of a magistrate, for which this *Centenier* received a severe reprimand from the Court and was ordered to pay costs. I speak of this irregular conduct on the part of the police to demonstrate to you that an illegal arrest is not acceptable to the Court. On 1st of June, 1799, Ann Baker and Margaret Platt were accused by the *Connétable* of St Mary of keeping an irregular house and of selling drink without a licence, and the Court ordered their arrest after a report. On 13th July, 1799, the *Connétable* of St Helier presented his report against a certain Nicolas Le Feuvre, for having kept his inn open after hours, and he was ordered to appear before the court to answer the accusation. Now you see, *Messieurs*, that in these various cases that I have just cited, the Court ordered the arrest of these persons after a complaint had been made against them by means of a *Connétable*'s report. On the 6th January, 1821, the *Connétable* of St Martin presented a report against Jean Bequet, because he permitted and encouraged children to drink and play cards in his inn, at all hours of the night, and this after the said *Connétable* had forbidden him to do so; the Court ordered him to appear before it; but there was no arrest, only an order, despite the grave charges and recidivism. Later, in 1840, M. le Connétable of St Helier, having received several complaints that pork butchers were killing their pigs in a courtyard in Ann Street, and a letter from neighbours complaining of this public nuisance, believed that he needed to place a report before the Court, which then ordered these butchers to appear to answer the complaints. The precedents that I have just cited therefore show that my argument is well-founded, that Le Gendre and his wife should have been proceeded against by means of a report and not by a summary arrest.

I know that there are cases in which there are arrests without such a report, when persons are caught *in flagrante*, and that there have been women so arrested for debauchery with soldiers in times of war[6]; but I think it suffices to demonstrate that the procedure has been used since 1799 in cases of persons accused of keeping *maisons de débauche*.

Now M. Le Cronier had been to Mulberry Cottage the previous Sunday and Thursday, and he said nothing about an arrest of the person whom he saw and to whom he spoke; but it was after he had received a letter from neighbours complaining that this house was a public nuisance that he thought of arresting her; for according to the testimony of M. Cousin, she said the evening before that if they came to take the clothes that belonged to her, she would defend herself; and I believe that these words that have been used against her will prove that it was only against the seizure of clothes that she proffered her threat; furthermore, there could not have been a disturbance or disorder at the house because on the Sunday M. Le Cronier had already placed the eleven girls who lived there in the hospital, and it has been proved to you that only two girls have lived there since.

Now did the *Centenier* Le Cronier have the right summarily to arrest the prisoner because of the letter that her neighbours had sent to the *Connétable*, or should this letter have been shown in Court, and a report entered against the people who kept the house? In the case of the butchers that I have just cited, they were merely ordered to attend Court and were not arrested, even after having shown their contempt for the police. Now I say that Le Cronier had no right to arrest the prisoner summarily; if he ordered Le Gendre to suppress the nuisance and Le Gendre had defied him, it would have been a completely different matter; but Le Gendre and his wife had received no intimation whatsoever that he was going to proceed against them if they didn't stop keeping this house as a public nuisance, as a public scandal; how could they have known this when he wrote to the *Connétable* about it only that morning? I maintain that this was a completely irregular manner of proceeding, that instead he should have produced this letter in Court and the Court should then have ordered the arrest of these people, or given them notice to attend.

It seems to me that there is another fact that you ought to consider carefully: it is odd that this step was taken only against the prisoner at the bar. According to the testimony of M. Manuel, they went to arrest only the wife, but why not the husband? When the late M. Le Cronier said that he was going to arrest her, she replied, 'My husband is not here.' Why did he not ask where he was? He went therefore to arrest only the woman, and I can demonstrate that when a man and wife keep a *maison de débauche*, it is not legal to proceed against only the wife, but only jointly with her husband. I know that in the minute produced in Court by M. *le Connétable* Le Sueur, Le Cronier's report must have been directed against husband and wife, but this minute was written by M. Le Sueur, and proves nothing of M. Le Cronier's intentions. It is perhaps true that, from the legal point of view, man and wife held their property separately; but, in a criminal endeavour, such separation cannot be allowed; the prisoner lives with her husband.

Now it remains for me to prove that if there is illegality in the manner of arrest by a public officer, and if in the course of such an arrest, he receives a fatal blow, this type of homicide must be considered only as a simple homicide or *manslaughter*.

I will now cite you a case in which a woman struck a blow with a knife under circumstances similar to the present case. On 14th September, 1779, Mary Haddy was accused at the Old Bailey of having caused the death of William Barnett. Now it appeared that this woman lived with a man called Parmello, and that a police officer called Protheroe, assisted by Barnett, went to arrest her, and at the moment they were making Parmello leave, this woman took a knife and struck Barnett under the arm, from which he died the following day. In many respects the facts in this case were highly analogous with those with which we are dealing today. The judges, believing that the *warrant* or order with which these officers were furnished was illegal, condemned her to imprisonment for eighteen months; it is said that they considered her crime to be one of *manslaughter*, the officers having entered illegally. If a person, at the moment a police officer was going to arrest him, said that it was illegal for him to be arrested, he would have known the consequences before killing that officer.

I say, therefore, that although the prisoner at the bar be morally guilty of the crime, she cannot be considered such in the eyes of the law, since she had been illegally arrested and if there had been a person guilty of keeping a house that was a public nuisance, it was clearly Pierre-Marie Le Gendre, not the prisoner at the bar.

Now, *Messieurs*, after having brought to your attention these precedents in defence of the unhappy prisoner at the bar, in support of the four points that I have enumerated in her defence, I ask you to examine all the evidence you have heard calmly and objectively. As for the evidence for the prosecution, I accept that the facts have been clearly and fully proven. You must have expressed your grief, with all your fellow-citizens, at the tragic event that has so unhappily occupied the attention of the entire island; but even if the prisoner at the bar were the vilest woman, the most execrable in the whole universe, if the law shows that there was illegality in the arrest, you would have to give her the benefit, for what is most certain is that she could have committed this crime in another way. If there had been premeditation, she could have committed it outside her house; but it was only when the *Centenier* Le Cronier entered her house and said that he was going to arrest her that she was impelled to this crime by the idea that she was going to be put in prison. I hope that you are going to base your verdict on the precedents I have given.

I submit to you a very important question. The prisoner at the bar acknowledges her crime – a grave crime, an execrable crime, I agree – but I hope that, after all the circumstances that I have enumerated, you will find some extenuation and render your verdict accordingly.

I find it difficult to believe that a jury of policemen, whose colleague had just been murdered, would have listened to Mr Hammond without mounting impatience or irritation. It was, after all, his contention that the victim was acting illegally himself, and no body of men likes to hear one of its members criticised in public (privately it is another matter altogether, of course).

The Attorney-General – the *Procureur-Général* – rose to refute Mr Hammond's arguments, and did so powerfully:

> *Monsieur le Bailli, Messieurs de Justice, et Messieurs les Membres de l'Enditement,* the prisoner at the bar stands before you under the weight of the most serious accusation that can weigh upon anybody: she is accused of having committed the crime of murder against the person of M. George Le Cronier, one of the *Centeniers* of the parish of St Helier, while fulfilling his duties: and this under the most aggravating circumstances.
>
> Now, *Messieurs,* in such cases as the present one, you must put aside all that you might have heard outside this court, and you must judge according to the evidence that has been presented to you, after the judicious observations of the defending counsel, and after the observations that I will have the honour to address to you on behalf of the Crown.
>
> It has been fully proved that the prisoner at the bar plunged a knife into the abdomen of M. Le Cronier, which caused his death; now you have to decide whether this crime is that of murder.
>
> I will put to you in few words the circumstances of this crime. 27th February last, M. *le Centenier* Le Cronier received an order to arrest this woman, who kept a brothel; he had at the same time received an order to do all that was in his power to suppress

these *maisons de débauche*. He went to Mulberry Cottage, occupied by the Le Gendre couple; it is well-established by the evidence of several witnesses that it was the prisoner at the bar who was the principal party, for she said to M. Philippe De Gruchy that M. Le Cronier had taken the girls from her and in so doing had destroyed all her trade and thus her means of subsistence. M. Le Cronier went to the prisoner's house, and told her that she would have to appear in court the next day, adding: 'If you don't give me security, I will be obliged to arrest you and put you in prison.'

Now in all this there is not a single act of M. Le Cronier's that could have provoked her: he didn't approach her, he didn't even touch her; but what does she do? She turns suddenly on him and plunges a knife into M. Le Cronier's stomach! I have said that it was a frightful crime, and I do not believe I could prove a more serious one; I believe that this is a case without parallel, a case without provocation.

But what proves that it was not M. Le Cronier's words that was the cause was that she had long had the intention that she put into execution. According to the facts so plainly proved and corroborated by various witnesses, it is obvious what she wanted to do to M. Le Cronier. She said it to M. Mannal, and gave the reason: it was because about seven years ago he had made her return a [purportedly stolen] bed that belonged to her. She declared to M. Cousin the evening before that if M. Le Cronier came to the house to search for the clothes of the girls in the hospital, '*I'll rip the b......'s guts*.'[7] Here is a clear indication of a determination to commit the crime.

There is also another circumstance that well merits your attention, it is the *carving knife*[8] of enormous size which caused the death; this knife, that previously had always been in the kitchen among the other knives, was on the day in question in the front room, ready to be used against any police officer who entered the house. All this proves that intention was clearly manifested not only by her acts, but by what she said. Her conversation with M. De Gruchy proves it in the most direct possible way; she said that he had taken her girls, that he had destroyed her trade, and that she would do him justice, even if it was at the doors of the courthouse. Her declarations to Émile Cousin and to M. Manuel prove that she committed the crime premeditatedly, not on the spur of the moment. Of this there cannot be the slightest doubt.

M. *l'Avocat* Hammond acknowledges that it was the prisoner at the bar who caused the death of M. Le Cronier; he bases his arguments on the illegality of M. Le Cronier's actions, of arresting a person who keeps a *maison de débauche* without a report having been entered against her; that M. Le Cronier entered the house without order or *warrant*[9], and therefore illegally; and that if a public servant enters a house illegally or without authority, and if he receives a fatal blow, the crime cannot be considered one of murder, but only of simple homicide or *manslaughter*. He has cited English authorities on this matter, and also a large number of precedents upon which he relies; now it remains to me to prove that the observations of M. *l'Avocat* Hammond are ill-founded, that there was nothing illegal about the arrest of this woman or in the conduct of M. *le Centenier* Le Cronier, and that our usage permitted it. He cited a case of 1796, in which a man called Hamon was accused of rape; this case has no analogy to the present one. As for the case of Mackenzie, an innkeeper who kept his inn open after hours, it is not he who is before you today. M. *l'Avocat* Hammond has also cited the case of Susanne Le Gros, found *in flagrante* with a soldier; this was a case of debauchery, her house wasn't known as a house of prostitution. Her case cannot be compared to the present one just because she committed an immoral act; and as for the case of the *Centenier* Nicolle who arrested Laurens and sent him to gaol, it proves nothing about what concerns us here today, because we know that if a police officer oversteps his powers, it is the Court that has the right to reprimand him or inflict another punishment that it thinks necessary. As for the case of Jean Bequet in 1821, for keeping his inn in an irregular fashion; that is prohibited by law and rendered him liable to a fine.

But I am going to quote a large number of cases in which the police proceeded in exactly the same way as M. Le Cronier on this occasion, and in almost identical circumstances. On the 19th January, 1799, Elizabeth Case was arrested by the police and presented in court for having kept debauched women and caused a public scandal. On 23rd February, 1799, Jean Mollet and Susanne Price, his wife, were arrested and presented in court for having given shelter to debauched women. Now these people had only given shelter to immoral women, not run a house of prostitution like that kept by the prisoner at the bar. On 3rd June, 1799, Rose

Casey was arrested by the *Connétable* of St Helier for keeping a disorderly house and put before the court. On 7th July, 1799, Jean Mollet and Susanne Price, his wife, were again before the court for keeping a disorderly house, having been arrested by the *Connétable*. On 17th October, 1800, Elizabeth Le Gallais was put before the court for having lodged persons and disturbed the public peace, having been arrested by the *Connétable*. In 1804 Ann Picot, wife of Adrien Joignant, was arrested and brought before the court for having lived a debauched life. On 27th April, 1807, Mary Drinkwater and Elizabeth Beer were arrested and put before the court for living in a disorderly way. On 21st August, 1813, Charles Marett, Charles Poingdestre, Susanne Michel and Marie Michel, living at Mont-a-l'Abbé, were arrested by the *Connétable* of St Helier and presented to the court for living a disorderly life and disturbing the public peace. Likewise, on October 29th 1819, Abraham Vidamour, his wife and Julie Camel; on February 25th, 1825, Elias Hutchings for having kept a disorderly house and sold drink without a licence. On 18th August, 1831, Jane Steel, Ann Scanlin and Jane Olden for having led a disorderly and scandalous life. On 17th April, Ellena Keating; on 1st December, 1832, Mary Henley; on 14th July, 1835, Richard Smith and his wife, Jane Smith; on November 5th, Mary Masters; on October 24th, Jeanne Patson, the widow Sullivan; on 9th December, 1839 Mary Rooks and Arthur Howe; January 13th, 1840, Jeanne Patson, the widow Sullivan; Mary Rider, the wife of Gillman, and others, were likewise presented in court by the *Connétable* of the parish of St Helier without any order by the chief Magistrate. You will therefore see that, at exactly the same period of the cases cited by M. *l'Avocat* Hammond, which were not numerous, the *Connétables* and *Centeniers* arrested several individuals for the same thing for which the prisoner at the bar was going to be arrested, and after the cases I have just cited in support of my contention, I am sure that you will see that, according to our custom, the *Connétables* have the right to arrest all persons whom they believe to be giving rise to public scandal. There is not a precedent because some *Connétables* believed that they had to present a report to the Court before arresting persons; it has to be judged case by case.

In this case, which was extremely serious, M. Le Cronier had the same right of arrest as the *Connétable*, and he acted as if he had been furnished with a warrant. I agree that, according to English law, if an officer is killed while making an illegal arrest, the crime is considered as voluntary homicide or *manslaughter*; but it is necessary to consider this case according to the evidence in the trial. It is allowed by Lord Hale[10] that the fact of killing an officer during an illegal arrest is considered *manslaughter*, but if there is *expressed malice*[11] it is murder. This principal is admitted by Hale, Foster and Archbold, three of the most eminent Commentators on criminal procedure.

Let us admit for a moment, what I am far from admitting, that M. Le Cronier did not have the right to enter the house, that he did not have the right to arrest the prisoner and take her to prison, if there are circumstances that prove premeditation, it is murder, even under English law.

Giving every possible advantage to the prisoner, to the observations of M. *l'Avocat* Hammond on the legality of the arrest, I maintain that there still exist proofs of *expressed malice* that completely change the case to one of murder.

There is another circumstance that you must examine, and that is that the knife was sharpened that very morning. For what purpose? One might perhaps say that there was no purpose, but then you consider all the circumstances, they form a chain of evidence. I think I can even say that the fact that she sharpened the knife proves that she did not find it sufficiently sharp to carry out her design, a design on M. Le Cronier that I cannot believe was other than premeditated. Her statements to Cousin and M. De Gruchy prove her firm intention to commit a crime against M. Le Cronier.

M. Hammond has told you that the husband was not arrested, and that it was he who ought to have been arrested, since it was he who rented the house. But this cannot extenuate the conduct of the prisoner; and I maintain that M. *le Centenier* Le Cronier had the right to arrest the prisoner and present her to the Court at the same time as his report, and that the arrest was legal.

M. *l'Avocat* Hammond claimed that the proceedings were founded on a letter from the neighbours, but it is obvious that this was not so. According to the evidence of M. Jean de Veulle, M. Le Cronier had received complaints against several such houses, which he had orders to suppress.

He cited a case to you which came before the Old Bailey in 1779, in which a man called Barnett who was accompanying a police officer was stabbed;

this case was a very old one, and required longer elucidation; it was said that the judges considered the crime that of *manslaughter*; but here we are in darkness. Now to base oneself on a case that is sixty years old, it is necessary to have the transcript before one, without which it is impossible to be guided by it in one's deliberations. If M. Hammond had cited more recent cases, it would have been worthier of your consideration.

I believe therefore that it is clear that M. Le Cronier was within his rights to make an arrest, and although it is claimed that the husband rather than the wife should have been arrested, this circumstance cannot in the slightest change the case, because this woman ought not to have deprived this man of his life in so frightful and atrocious a way.

I believe it is my duty, in the interests of society, to make these remarks to you; but if you have any doubts about the evidence furnished, you will give the accused their benefit. You must not, by an ill-judged mercy, acquit the prisoner charged with so atrocious a crime, but you must render your verdict according to the evidence presented to you, in order to maintain the good order of society and respect for the laws and those charged with enforcing them. You must examine calmly and objectively the evidence and the arguments presented by the defender of the accused. You must fulfil the painful duty with which you are entrusted, and say conscientiously, without hatred, fear or favour, whether you believe the prisoner at the bar to be more innocent than guilty, or more guilty than innocent, of the crime of which she is accused.

The arguments over, the Bailiff summed up (there is no transcript of what he said) and then the jury retired. It took it exactly 11 minutes to come to a unanimous verdict: that Mme. Le Gendre was more guilty than innocent. Mr Hammond immediately demanded recourse to *la Grande Enquête du pays*, a demand that was acceded to. It took place three days later.

XII

This trial was not the first at which Mr Hammond had been called upon to defend the *woman* (as she was sometimes known) Le Gendre. He had defended her against the charge of receiving stolen goods in 1837, and Mme Le Gendre had probably never lived a life of deep respectability. Under the headline *Brutal Assault*, the *Jersey Argus* for August 22, 1836, reported:

> John Le Roux, Thomas Craig, Gallichan, and Jane Moore, who, in broad day light, on Sunday the 7th *inst.*, entered the house of Mrs Mary Le Noble, and committed a violent and ruffian-like assault on her person, by breaking two of her ribs with a mop, knocking out four of her front teeth, and dislocating her shoulder, besides breaking several panes of glass in her house, were again this day brought before the Royal Court to hear witnesses at the suit of the Crown. Jane Moore, it appeared, committed the lesser assault by arming herself with stones, with which she smashed several panes of glass, and thus proved herself at least a friend of the glazier. Having submitted to the judgement of the Court, this Amazon was condemned to fifteen days' imprisonment, in consideration of the confinement she has already endured. Her other accomplices were remanded...

What subsequently happened to them I have been unable to discover. But without wishing in any way to exonerate or exculpate those who assaulted her, I cannot help but suspect that they had had a grudge against her, and that this grudge arose from her mode of life, in which violent quarrels arose more frequently even than among newspaper editors in Jersey.[1] Her loss of teeth (never referred to during her trial) must have rendered her unattractive, at least until she replaced them by false ones – if she did in fact do so.

Madame Le Gendre appeared before the courts on Wednesday, 19 April, 1837, in the company of George Le Gros (her brother-in-law), Christian Cooper, Henry Connell *aka* Coleman, and the woman Matthews, charged with having stolen and received stolen cheeses, bottles of wine, shoes, etc., from several houses.[2] Apparently, Mr Hammond pleaded 'eloquently' on her behalf, saying that there was no proof that she knew that the stolen goods found in her possession had been stolen, but the judges had no difficulty in dismissing this as fanciful, and sentenced her to one month's imprisonment, which the prison records for 1837 in the Jersey Archive establish that she spent in solitary confinement. Conditions in the prison at that time were probably very harsh, for in 1845 new regulations were issued.[3] They were prefaced by the following words:

> Whereas the management of Her Majesty's Gaol in the Island of Jersey is now and for some time past has been very defective…

The new regulations suggest that there had been considerable corruption. The gaoler, they said (p. 14):

> … shall not be concerned in any occupation or trade; he is not to sell or let, (nor is any person in trust for him to sell or let), or have any benefit from the sale or letting of any article, or dealing with, any prisoner; he shall not let for hire to any person any room… he shall not directly or indirectly have any interest in any contract or agreement for the supply of the prison.

This, it seems, turned out to be rather easier to lay down than enforce. Idly going through some later documents relating to the history of crime in Jersey, I discovered that the last man publicly executed in the British Isles was in Jersey, a Joseph Philip Le Brun, who was hanged in 1875 for murder. Shortly afterwards, a crudely-printed broadsheet was published with the title *The Jersey Menagerie*. Under the title *Questions* it asked:

> Who allowed the Keeper of the House of Correction to attend races, poultry shows, and other entertainments? Ask John Coutanche and Co. Who profited by the high price at which tobacco was sold to prisoners on the quiet? Ask John Countanche and Co.

Turning its attention to the execution of Le Brun, it stated:

> In the August accounts of the prison we find re J. Ph. Le Brun: -
> For timber (scaffold) £30.11.6
> For timber and labour (scaffold) £11.12.2
> Mr Jackson – Labour, etc., for ditto £12.3.7
> (Total:) £54.7.3
> There are other items, re Le Brun, to which we will call public attention. It costs a good penny to hang a man in Jersey jail!

Of course, an accusation of corruption is not itself proof of corruption; it might just as well be the product of malice; but it would be surprising if, in a society as small and intimately interconnected as Jersey's, favours were never done by officials to contractors of their personal acquaintance.

The new regulations state (p.44) that prisoners 'in separate confinement shall be furnished with the means of moral and religious instruction, and with suitable books.' Whether this was already done in 1837, I cannot say; if it was, it seemed to have had little effect on Marie Le Gendre's moral development. Her reading of the Bible in prison nine years later also had a severely time-limited effect upon her morals. Sir John Le Couteur's diary mentions that Madame Le Gendre's husband had always found her of violent and ungovernable temper.

XIII

The *Grande Enquête du pays* duly took place the following Tuesday. In a *Grande Enquête*, as I have said, the 24 jurors were allowed to read the written transcript of the evidence, but not to hear it for themselves; they did listen, however, to the two advocates repeating their final arguments. Much to everyone's surprise, and to many people's dismay, the jury found Madame Le Gendre not guilty of murder, but only of voluntary homicide. This was because, while 19 voted that she was guilty of murder, five voted that she was not. Voluntary homicide was thus the highest common denominator between the two factions of the jury.

There was widespread public outrage at the verdict. It set off a violent controversy between various newspapers, and the jurors who had voted for murder put up public notices to the effect that they had done so, and naming the jurors who had voted against. Mr Hammond had obviously done his job very well.

It may be doubted, however, that it was his arguments that won the day, and secured for Marie Le Noble a punishment not of death by hanging, but of transportation for life to Van Diemen's Land.[1] My admiration of Advocate Hammond notwithstanding, despite my respect for him as the kind of honest and upright lawyer (yes, such beings exist, and I have known many of them) to whom you might entrust your case in the certain knowledge that he would do his best for you, I do not see how any objective person could have come to the conclusion that he had had the best of the closing arguments. This was not his fault, of course; there is only so far that even the finest rhetorician can push a weak argument, or a listener can accept it. Madame Le Gendre had threatened 'to rip Le Cronier's guts'; she had a carving knife sharpened and laid it by in an unaccustomed room, the very room to which Le Cronier would almost certainly come if he came to Mulberry

Cottage at all; and then she did 'rip his guts', exactly as she had said she would. Thereafter, she would almost certainly have stabbed another man, quite possibly to death, if he had not managed to run away, and she threatened to deal with 'any other gentlemen who came' in the same way.

Her threat to stab Le Cronier and her preparation of the knife with which to do so dispose of any claim that her act was the result of provocation or was unpremeditated, even in the lay, let alone in the legal, sense of the word 'unpremeditated'. Malice aforethought, to exist, does not require long planning ahead, as in most crime novels, but only the intention to kill or seriously to injure, or extreme recklessness as to whether an act will result in death; the required degree of intention can be virtually instantaneous. And nobody does what Madame Le Gendre did to Monsieur Le Cronier while wishing the victim well. No one is so ignorant of trauma medicine that he does not know that sticking a large knife into someone's guts is unlikely to be life-preserving. As to Advocate Hammond's argument that the offence of killing an official while he makes an illegal arrest (even if it is accepted that Le Cronier *was* making an illegal arrest, which seems to be highly debatable) is manslaughter not murder, it is valid only in the absence of pre-expressed malice. And if anyone ever bore malice, it was Madame Le Gendre.

What, then, was on the mind of the five jurors who voted for acquittal from the charge of murder? Not Advocate Hammond's arguments, surely: it was rather the prospect of the death penalty. Executions were still public in those days, and the prospect of hanging a woman in front of a large mob was one at which the jurors (I surmise) flinched. No doubt some would find this mark of gallantry stained by the original sin of patriarchalism – women demand the right to be publicly executed along with the best, or the worst, of them! – but there is no denying that, in this instance, Victorian male delicacy, the jury being all-male, worked in favour of Madame Le Gendre.

It is true that, the existence of the death penalty notwithstanding, most murderers in the British Isles were not executed, publicly or in any other way. There were 'at least' 60 murders known in Jersey from 1805 to 1905, excluding infanticides.[2] I have been able to trace four executions on the island during that period.[3] Although the death penalty was passed automatically for the crime of murder, the sentence was commuted in 93 per cent of cases in Jersey, assuming my figures for murders and executions are accurate. Thus, the deterrent effect of the death penalty, if there was one, was exercised not by the fact that one *would* be executed if one was found guilty of murder, but by the fact that one *might* be. Quite apart from the question of justice (it is an uncomfortable fact that some murders seem more heinous than others), this was good psychology, for possibilities exercise a more powerful effect upon the imagination than certainties.

However, in the case of Madame Le Gendre, it is difficult to believe that, had she been found guilty of murder, commutation would have followed. The murder of policemen has always been thought particularly serious, because it strikes at society's thin blue line between order and anarchy. The Homicide Act of 1957, which was a halfway house to the abolition of the death penalty in Britain, retained it for certain restricted categories of murder, among them the murder of a policeman. If Madame Le Gendre had been found guilty, then, she would have hanged, and in public.

As it happens, Sir John Le Couteur, to whom it would have fallen to supervise the execution of Madame Le Gendre had it taken place, was one of the nine witnesses to appear before the Select Committee of the House of Lords set up in 1856 'to take into consideration the present mode of carrying into effect capital punishments,' that is to say, public executions. It was this committee that recommended that, thenceforth, executions be held in the comparative privacy of prison grounds. In his evidence, Le Couteur mentions the case of Madame Le Gendre without naming her:

LE COUTEUR: Executions [in Jersey] formerly took place on the Gallows Hill, which is a very conspicuous spot, overlooking the town; and from there the execution could be seen by almost the whole population of the island, and it was made a spectacle and a sight of, producing that effect on the minds of the people which I considered an execution should not have. In consequence, I wrote to the Secretary of State, to request him, should an execution took place, to allow it to take place within the walls of the prison, on the ground that it would have a greater moral effect than if made a public spectacle of.

CHAIRMAN: Was there not a female under sentence of death at that time?

LE COUTEUR: I wrote in anticipation of an execution taking place. The woman your Lordship refers to was found guilty of manslaughter.[4]

The Secretary of State replied to Le Couteur that he could hang the condemned in the prison, provided that the hanging was visible from at least one street, that is to say it was public.

But there was also feeling in 19th century Jersey against the death penalty in general, not just against the death penalty for women or public executions. The French exile, L. D. Hurel, whose *La lyre exilée* has already been quoted, was outraged by the verdict acquitting Madame Le Gendre of the most serious crime, and finding her guilty only of a lesser crime. A prolific employer of exclamation marks, one feels that he has difficulty in containing his indignation, and that without the relief afforded him by punctuation he might have exploded from his own pent-up emotion. Here he is on the outcome of the trial:

The surprising and unpopular verdict that caused
stupefaction to the inhabitants of Jersey, declared
*the woman Le Gendre innocent of the crime of the murder
of le Centenier Le Cronier!!* Yes, *innocent!* in spite of the
fact that it had been in an incontestable manner that
no murder was ever committed more horribly cold-
bloodedly, and without any provocation! Yes, *innocent!*
despite the amount of evidence proving murder,
despite the admissions of the eloquent defender of *la*
Le Gendre, and those of the monster herself!

Hurel must have known that any other verdict would have
meant a death sentence for Le Gendre, yet the very next poem to
the *Chant funebre sur la mort de M. George Le Cronier* is titled *La peine de
mort*, an appeal for the commutation of Thomas Nicolle's sentence
of death for the murder at Seward's café of Simon Levi, in the
month before Madame Le Gendre killed Monsieur Le Cronier.
By the time the poem was published, of course, the sentence had
already been commuted; and, like the *Chant funebre*, it came with
an explanatory note:

This piece of verse was composed with the purpose
of causing the death sentence that was hanging
over Thomas Nicolle to be set aside, and with the
purpose of bringing consolation to a numerous and
honourable family of this island, in demonstrating
that the death penalty is against religion, morality
and reason; that it is unworthy of Christian and
civilised peoples, that it remedies nothing and
corrects nobody. The *harsh* verdict that condemned
the unhappy Nicolle to the ultimate penalty, excited
the surprise and pity of many people; pity above all
for his poor pregnant wife, already the mother of
several children, for this unfortunate woman whose

real and great pain placed at death's door, several doctors despairing her life. And it had been virtually proved that Nicolle was *almost drunk and all but mad*, and that he had been struck an hour before the catastrophe which took place in the Royal Square, at the café Seward! And notwithstanding the absence of direct proofs against Nicolle, since no one ever said: It was he who was M. Levi's murderer, I saw him shoot his gun through the shutters of the café Seward.

In all this, in my opinion, there was room to apply *extenuating circumstances* with a thousand times more reason than in the case of Le Gendre! what a shocking contrast between these two verdicts! But happily for Thomas Nicolle, and above all for his poor wife, the noble and generous efforts of M. Hammond, who had defended him with such warmth and eloquence before the *enditement* of St Helier and before the *Grande Enquête du pays*, were crowned with complete success. Queen Victoria spared the life of Thomas Nicolle!

As for the poem itself, it rehearses all the arguments not only against the death penalty, but against public execution.[5] It is less liberally sown with exclamation marks than the *Chant funebre*, perhaps because of the abstract nature of the subject matter, only 23 in 117 lines; but it is passionate nonetheless.

Public execution fails in its purpose:

> Que vous sert d'ordonner un odieux trépas?
> Vous effrayez en vain: vous ne corrigez pas.[6]

It is useless:

Mais il faut un example... Eh! quoi! l'aspect
horrible
D'un échefaud sanglant a-t-il jamais changé
Le coeur du scélerat dans le crime engagé?
Non; ce drame hideux, ce spectacle terrible,
Est un beau jour pour lui; son coeur l'aime; il lui
plait.[7]

The spectacle is a savage and degrading one:

N'écoutez point les voeux d'une foule écumante,
Qui, trop semblable au tigre, est avide de sang,
Qui, pour voir de plus pres une mort infamante,
Avant l'heure retient sa place au premier rang.[8]

The death penalty is hypocritical judicial murder:

La loi reconnait donc des meurtres légitimes!
Mais ces meurtres légaux en sont-ils moins des
crimes?
En vain l'humanité fait entendre sa voix;
La loi défend le meurtre et l'ordonne a la fois![9]

The death penalty is against religion because:

La vie est a Dieu seul; il l'a tient dans ses mains;
Seul, il doit disposer des malheureux humains.[10]

What is more, there was the possibility of hanging the wrong
man or woman:

Vos arrêts bien souvent ont frappé l'innocence!
Comment osez-vous donc, sans horreur, sans
effroi,

De la peine de mort prononcer la sentence![11]

Even if the executed person is guilty, the innocent suffer:

Vous ordonnez sa mort… mais ses enfants, sa
femme,
Vous les tuez aussi c'est tuer l'innocent.[12]

Although the poem was written before Thomas Nicolle's
sentence was commuted, Hurel obviously added some lines as
a dithyramb to Queen Victoria's clemency (actually Sir James
Graham's). In fact, it almost seems as if the death penalty does
serve *one* useful purpose as far as the author is concerned:

Qu'il est beau! qu'il est grand! Ce privilege auguste
D'arracher a la mort un pauvre condamné…[13]
'What a most glorious right was given to you, O
Kings!'

And Hurel advises them to follow in Victoria's merciful
footsteps, whereupon they will be blessed and adored. The death
penalty is like whipping: it is nice when it is stopped.

The arguments put forward by Hurel against it were old ones,
and were to be repeated in Britain for a further century until the
death penalty was finally abolished. Hurel's protest against the
degrading spectacle of public execution became redundant or
obsolete relatively soon, but executions continued in 'private', as it
were, behind prison walls, in what were colloquially known in the
trade as 'topping sheds.' How good were Hurel's arguments?

I have found in discussing the death penalty that one soon
enters a morass of conflicting emotion, argument and counter-
argument, logic and illogic, fact and rumour of fact. Recently, for
example, the subject came up at a dinner I attended. I said that
it seemed to me that the strongest argument against the death

penalty, the one that came nearest to being morally decisive (and one used by Hurel), was that the innocent were sometimes executed, and that this had happened in all jurisdictions.

One of the people attending the dinner, a proponent of the death penalty, said – with evident passion – that he could easily refute my argument. The number of people killed by murderers after conviction for a first murder, he said, outnumbered by far the number of people wrongly executed.

Is this right?

If it were, it would depend upon utilitarianism being right: on that which is moral being that which produces the greatest happiness of the greatest number, or (in this case) the smaller number of deaths. On a utilitarian view[14], it would be morally permissible, indeed obligatory, to be prepared to execute the wrong person if by doing so the total number of deaths by murder is reduced. It is to turn Voltaire's quip about the execution of Admiral Byng, that it was carried out *'pour encourager les autres'*[15], into a principle of jurisprudence. And this surely must be wrong: for although most wrongful executions, at least in civilised jurisdictions, have been carried out by mistake rather than deliberately, it would make deliberate wrongful execution permissible at least occasionally or in the 'right' circumstances. This is repellent to our sense of natural justice, as well as likely in practice to lead to the grossest oppression and cruelty, for it would be virtually impossible, once permitted, to limit wrongful executions (or wrongful punishment of any kind) to precisely the number or amount necessary to have the desired effect. Far from justifying capital punishment, the argument disproves utilitarianism, at least as a universal metaphysical grounding for morality.

In the second place, the argument is less impressive on purely empirical grounds than it might at first appear. Since the abolition of the death penalty in the 1960s, about four murders a year have been committed in Britain by those who have already been convicted of murder.[16] But in Britain of the first half of the 20th

101

century, as in Jersey of the 19th, only a minority of convicted murderers were executed: about one in 12, which is to say that, assuming that convicted murders who go on to commit a second murder would have been executed at the same rate as murderers who do not[17], one murder every four years would have been prevented by the continuation of the death penalty. In those four years, there would have been in excess of 36 executions. If the rate of judicial error was one per cent, then for every three murders prevented there would have be one execution of an innocent man. There is no indisputable answer to the question of whether the light of three murders prevented is worth the candle of one execution of an innocent man; suffice it to say that for most people, the idea of the state killing an innocent man (that is to say, innocent of what he is charged with, not necessarily innocent in any other way) is peculiarly abhorrent.

But Hurel's other arguments are less solid, and one or two are bad. Whether or not the death penalty acts as a deterrent is still a matter of discussion. It is far from certain that it does not; Hurel was going beyond the evidence when he said that no criminal was ever put off by the death penalty.

While it is true that a wife and children would probably have been distraught at the prospect of the death by execution of their husband and father, Hurel asserts in his poem that severe punishment was perfectly appropriate in cases of murder; and at the time in which he was writing, the punishment that was the alternative to the death penalty was transportation overseas for life, without benefit of accompaniment by wife and children.[18] The joy of commutation could hardly have been long-lasting, then; if there was any love between man and wife (as there appears to have been in the case of Mr and Mrs Nicolle), transportation for life would have caused almost as much heartache as execution. Thomas Nicolle was not going to be a father to the unborn child his wife was carrying whether he was executed or transported for life – or for that matter imprisoned within the British Isles for many years.

As to forgiveness, whose virtues Hurel extols, I have always felt slightly uneasy about it when it is exercised by a third party who has not himself been wronged by the person he forgives. I can forgive what is done to me if I so choose, if I find it in my heart to do so, but by what right do I forgive what is done to another? That kind of forgiveness easily degenerates into mere sentimentality and, worse still, into moral exhibitionism.

The distinction that Hurel draws between the degree of culpability of the two killers, Thomas Nicolle on the one hand, and Madame Le Gendre on the other, seems to me far too great and without real moral foundation. Madame Le Gendre was not an admirable figure, even if she was a spirited one, but Nicolle was far from admirable either. By all accounts, he neglected his family, preferring the amusements of drinking and gambling to attention to his business, a preference which might have been his affair alone had he had no family obligations, but which took on quite another hue when it blighted the lives of others.

It is difficult not to see the workings of social prejudice in Hurel's defence of Nicolle, coming as he did (unlike Madame Le Gendre) from an 'honourable' family. From a certain point of view, this provenance might have been supposed to heighten his culpability, in so far as he had received an education that had given him the opportunity to do better. There were thus fewer mitigating circumstances for his option for drinking and gambling than for Madame Le Gendre's option for brothel-keeping.

Hurel says that there is no certain evidence that Nicolle actually committed the murder, but the circumstantial evidence was so strong that it amounted to proof beyond reasonable doubt. He had a drunken quarrel in a bar with the owner; he had a fight with the owner; a few minutes later a gun was fired into the bar, and a man was seen running away, who entered the accused man's abode. No one else entered that abode, and the following day he was found with a gun that had recently discharged bullets similar to those found in the dead man's body. Nor did he protest his innocence after the verdict.

The existence of only circumstantial evidence of a crime is not a mitigation of it, as Hurel seems to suggest. If the circumstantial evidence is sufficient to convict, as it certainly was in Nicolle's case, the crime is as serious (or trivial) as it would have been had there been more direct evidence against the culprit. And Hurel seems to contradict his own doubts about Nicolle's guilt when he says in his defence, as mitigation, that he was half-drunk and half-mad at the time. If he was not guilty of the crime, his state of mind when it was committed is irrelevant; the fact that Hurel brings it up suggests that he knew perfectly well that Nicolle committed it.

Hurel also implies that Nicolle was provoked; the bar or café-owner, Seward, hit him a few minutes before he shot Simon Levi dead through the shutters of Seward's bar. Leaving aside who was responsible for the quarrel that ended in Seward striking him, the fact that Nicolle went home afterwards, fetched a gun, and returned to the bar, where he discharged it several times, rules out the legal defence of provocation and the moral one too. It is surely a moral as well as a legal requirement that people should not react in this way; Nicolle was not acting in the heat of the moment, but in a planned and deliberate way.

Did his having been 'half-drunk' excuse him, or mitigate his offence? Would the excuse or mitigation have been stronger if Nicolle had been much more drunk than he actually was?[19] It has long been the principle of the law that voluntary intoxication is not a mitigating circumstance, much less an excuse, where a serious crime has been committed, and in this it is surely correct. To allow drunkenness to be a mitigating circumstance or an excuse for serious crime is to invite drunks not to control themselves, by letting them know in advance that they will be treated leniently if they misbehave. Nor is drunkenness a moral, though not a legal, excuse: for, contrary to what many people suppose, the release of violent propensities is not (except in rare cases) a simply physiological effect of alcohol.[20] If it were, it would be reprehensible for someone of those propensities to have taken it at all, except – possibly – on the first occasion in life when it was taken, which it clearly was not in Nicolle's case.

But what if Nicolle were an alcoholic, would that affect the matter, morally if not legally? Let us put the case at its strongest, and suppose for a moment what is clearly not true: that alcoholism is a disease in which a person is genetically-determined when he takes his first drink of alcohol to drink to excess ever afterwards, being quite unable to control himself, either as to whether to drink or as to the amount that he drinks; furthermore, all that he does under the influence of drink is the physiological consequence of that drink, and not a matter of choice or decision-making on his part.

If this were true in Nicolle's case, it would indeed lessen his moral responsibility for what he did; but it would hardly have the liberal penal consequences that Hurel clearly favours, because it would mean that Nicolle was, and would remain all his life, an extremely dangerous man, at least if he continued to live in a society in which alcohol were freely available: for not only would he be unable to refrain from drinking it, but he would be unable to prevent the consequences of his having done so. If he really couldn't help himself drinking and going round shooting people while under the influence, the appropriate preventive action is obvious: he should be locked up for the rest of his life in an alcohol-free establishment.

But in fact this view of alcoholism is nonsense. Even drunkards do not lose their ability to choose.[21] If it were true, no alcoholic could ever stop drinking, and millions *have* stopped drinking. The British law said for a long time that being drunk is an excuse or mitigating circumstance for a crime if, and only if, the person could not have refrained from taking the first drink of the day[22]: but, to quote Betsy Prig with regard to Mrs Harris, I don't believe there's no sich a person. And if there were, he would be very dangerous.

Was Nicolle half-mad, and if so did it make him less responsible for his actions than was Madame Le Gendre for hers? The commutation of his sentence mentioned the possibility of mental alienation for the reprieve, but this was inconsistent with the facts of the case. Certainly, Nicolle could not have claimed a defence of insanity under English law, a law which was clarified, or at least laid down, less than three years before his crime, in the famous case of M'Naghten.

Daniel M'Naghten (1813 – 1865) was a wood-turner who suffered from the delusion that the Tory party was persecuting him.[23] He shot and killed Edward Drummond, the personal secretary of the Prime Minister, Sir Robert Peel, in the mistaken belief that Drummond was Peel himself. M'Naghten made a brief statement at Bow Street Magistrates' Court, saying, 'The Tories in my native city have compelled me to do this. They follow me wherever I go, and have entirely destroyed my peace of mind. It can be proved by evidence. That is all I have to say.' At his Old Bailey trial, M'Naghten, when asked how he pleaded, guilty or not guilty, replied 'I was driven to desperation by persecution,' and when asked again whether he was guilty or not guilty, said 'I am guilty of firing.' The defence argued that M'Naghten was mad, and produced several eminent medical experts to prove it. The prosecution offered no medical evidence in rebuttal, and M'Naghten was found not guilty by reason of insanity. He was then taken off to Bedlam.

But the verdict of not guilty alarmed both Queen Victoria and the general public, and the judges were asked to produce a statement of the law of insanity in relation to criminal acts. When did insanity become a complete defence against an accusation? M'Naghten, after all, had gone about his ordinary business in a normal way; passing him in the street, you would not have known that he was mad. How extensive or complete did madness have to be before it excused a criminal act?

The judges returned the famous *M'Naghten Rules*, which for at least a hundred years influenced jurisprudence in all English-speaking jurisdictions, though they – the rules – were often criticised for their lack of theoretical clarity and rigour. Doctors disliked them because legal categories did not coincide with medical ones, a foolish criticism because the purposes of the law are different from those of medicine. But despite (or is it because of?) their lack of clarity and rigour, the rules served their purpose well, which was to be humane without sentimentality. The most famous sentence in the rules, one which is known by heart to all who have occasion to deal with the insanity defence of alleged murderers, is:

> To establish a defence on the ground of insanity it must be clearly proved, that, at the time of committing the act, the party accused was labouring under such a defect of reason from disease of the mind, as not to know the nature and quality of the act he was doing, or if he did know it, that he did not know that what he was doing was wrong.

On most interpretations of the M'Naghten rules, M'Naghten himself was not legally insane; though his delusion would and should have been a mitigation of his crime, it was not a complete defence (as insanity would have been). In other words, the jury was mistaken, in retrospect, to have acquitted him on the grounds of insanity. He should have been found guilty, and his sentence commuted.

A delusion is a complete defence under the M'Naghten rules if the content of the delusion would have excused the act *had the delusion been true*. Suppose, for example, that M'Naghten had believed that Drummond, being party to the conspiracy against him, was about to shoot him dead: his act, if Drummond had really been about to shoot him, would then have been one of self-defence, which is a complete defence to the charge of murder. But merely being spied upon or followed is not a legal defence to the charge of murder of the person doing or ordering it.

Alternatively, if M'Naghten had thought that Drummond was suffering from lead deficiency, and that insinuating a bullet into him was the way medicinally to supply the lead that he lacked, he would have been not guilty by reason of insanity, for then he would not have known the nature and quality of his act.

In fact, there is a scholastic quality, at least nowadays, to the whole argument, because in practice the fate of someone who is found not guilty by reason of insanity, and one who is found guilty of manslaughter by reason of partial insanity, tends to be very similar: incarceration in a high security psychiatric facility until he is judged to be cured and therefore no further risk to society. However, the man found not guilty by reason of insanity has no criminal record, for he has committed no crime, unlike the person found guilty of manslaughter by reason of partial insanity.[24]

Regardless, the sentence of death passed on Thomas Nicolle was commuted in part because there was an aura of madness hanging over him. Once again the excellent Mr Hammond did his best in court for his client, conscientiously calling upon those who could testify to behaviour that most people would consider mad. It is impossible at this distance to suggest what ailed Nicolle, that is to say into what Procrustean diagnostic bed he would now, in our enlightened times, be fitted by doctors; diagnosis on written evidence alone is always hazardous, and in this case the written evidence is not very extensive. A pamphlet or chapbook written in Jersey in 1846, titled *Vie, proces, jugement et condamnation de Thomas Nicolle, trouvé coupable du crime du meurtre, sur la personne de Sieur Abraham alias Simon Levi, et de tentative de meurtre contre Miss Mary Cook, crime qui eut lieu au café Seward, Place Royale a Jersey* (Life, Trial, Verdict and Sentence of Thomas Nicolle, Found Guilty of the Crime of Murder of the Person of Mr Abraham, *alias* Simon Levi, and of the Attempted Murder of Miss Mary Cook, which Took Place

at the Café Seward, Royal Square, Jersey), suggests that he was a
bad lot from the beginning: that he scorned the education he had
received, no sacrifice spared, from his parents, in favour of gaming
and debauchery. According to the pamphlet, Nicolle had been
before the magistrates several times before, but he had scorned
their 'paternal reproaches', returning as a dog to his vomit. But
such pamphlets or chapbooks were always eager to use cases for
the purposes of moral exhortation. Another such pamphlet or
chapbook, published in Jersey in 1846 by one P. Vautier, titled
*Récit d'évenemens affreux qui ont lieu dans la fin de l'année mil huit cent
quarante-cinq et au commencement de mil huit cent quarante-six* (Account
of the Frightful Events which Took Place at the End of the Year
1845 and the Beginning of 1846) suggests that some good might
come out of the events at the Café Seward, in as much as Miss
Cook, having narrowly escaped death, might turn to God, the
authorities' eyes might be opened to the wickedness of St Helier,
male heads of families might learn not to spend their money in
cafés, the number of inns might be reduced and their hours of
opening limited, especially on Sundays, and the police might learn
that in the midst of life we – or, more particularly, they – are in
death. Vautier wrote an annual series of such documents, reflecting
on the worst events in Jersey in the previous year, pointing always
more or less the same moral: which perhaps is not surprising, or as
unsophisticated as it seems, because the cardinal sins and virtues
remain the same at all times and in all places, which is why they
are cardinal.

Though Mr Hammond did indeed produce evidence of mental
alienation, as it was then called, at some time in Nicolle's past, this
again was so much dust in the jury's eyes. What counted in law was
his state of mind at the time he committed the act, and there is not
the slightest indication that his actions were the result of anything
other than drunken quarrelsomeness. He went, drunk, into the café,
had a quarrel with the owner about a bill, got mildly beaten for his
pains, and returned with a gun which he shot through the shutters

of the café in a fury of revenge. Interestingly, he was examined by doctors in Millbank, the London penitentiary to which he was sent in preparation for his permanent transportation, who found in him no signs of mental alienation.[25] Nor had there been any signs of it while he was in prison in Jersey. I think it quite probable that most of Nicolle's odd conduct was the consequence of his immoderate consumption of alcohol, with its well-known propensity to licence, explain and excuse behaviour that would not be tolerable, even to the person himself, when sober. But I cannot be sure of this: some of those who testified to his mental alienation said that they had never seen him drunk.

At any rate, it is clear that Nicolle's state of mind at the time of his act was not an extenuation of it.

The other circumstance that the Home Secretary took into account was that Nicolle did not intend to kill Simon Levi when he shot the gun. He had no quarrel with Levi; if he was aiming at anyone, he was aiming at Seward. But it is no defence to the charge of murder that one did not intend to kill the person one did actually kill, because one was aiming at someone else. And it would also be no defence that Nicolle did not even intend to kill Seward, but only frighten him; for shooting eight bullets blindly into a café that you know to have several people inside it is extreme recklessness, if anything could ever be extreme recklessness.

In short, it is difficult to see anything like an extenuating or mitigating circumstance in Nicolle's case, any more than in Madame Le Gendre's case, and as with her case, the commutation of sentence was not really based upon any arguments that could be produced in his favour, or arguments that were not easily refutable. It is difficult to resist the conclusion, then, that the commutation was caused by a queasiness or unease about the death penalty itself, which – if it was to be used at all – was to be used sparingly. One is inclined to imagine Victorian penology as being harsh, vengefully and unthinkingly retributive; but the cases of Nicolle and Madame Le Gendre suggest quite otherwise.

Also of interest considering that, nearly a century later, the Nazis occupied the Channel Islands and the authorities were sometimes charged by later historians with having co-operated unduly in anti-Semitic measures, mainly because of their own anti-Semitic prejudices, is the fact that there was not the slightest hint of anti-Semitism in the official, journalistic or legal response to Simon Levi's murder: that, for example, his killer had been leniently dealt with because his victim was considered of less account than anybody else.

XIV

The M'Naghten case, and the legal rules concerning insanity to which it gave rise, were not relevant to that of Thomas Nicolle, despite the suspicion of his mentally unstable conduct in the past (a man is not held to be always mad because he has once been mad); but, strangely enough, the case was relevant in one respect to that of John Noon, who stabbed Thomas Hodge to death. And that respect was incompetence in the medical aid given to the dying men.

Drummond, the man shot by M'Naghten, did not die at once, but only after four days. He managed to walk immediately after he was shot, though with assistance; his wound was initially not thought to be dangerous and he was expected to recover. The surgeons who attended him decided to remove the bullet from his body; after that, he developed a fever, for which he was copiously bled. According to a pamphlet published by the most prominent British opponent of supposedly therapeutic blood-letting, Dr Samuel Dickson[1], Drummond died of his treatment rather than of his original injury. The pamphlet was titled *What Killed Mr. Drummond, the Lead or the Lancet?*[2] The lead was the bullet, and the lancet was the implement with which a vein or, as in Drummond's case, the temporal artery, was opened to let blood out.

Dickson, who published under the pseudonym of 'An Old Army Surgeon', denied that there had been any necessity to remove the bullet. At post mortem, it was discovered to have injured no vital organ, and Dickson stated:

> Men have lived and are now living, in whose bodies
> balls [bullets] have remained for years without
> occasioning half the pain [the extraction] must
> have caused.[3]

The initial wound had not given rise to shock, the amount of blood found post mortem in the thoracic cavity and abdomen being quite small, while fever followed the removal of the bullet. It was quite possibly the removal rather than the bullet itself that caused the fever because the surgeons initially looked for it in the wrong place, that is to say around the entry wound, and antisepsis was unknown at that time. Poking about in wounds with unsterilised instruments and dirty hands was almost bound to result in infection, and when the latter did indeed supervene, the treatment was drastic. And what was the treatment, asked Dickson?

> Blood-letting repeated and re-repeated – *twice* in one day! – leeches in numbers were also applied and bleeding again resorted to. The temporal artery was in the first instance opened! – and the result of all – DEATH![4]

It is, of course, impossible to be categorical about the matter, but it seems at least likely that Dickson was right: Drummond would have had a better chance of survival if he had received no medical attention at all. And interestingly, one of the surgeons attending him was Mr Bransby Cooper, nephew of the great surgeon, Sir Astley Cooper, whom we met above. A few years earlier, Bransby Cooper had brought an action for libel against Thomas Wakley, the editor of *The Lancet*, the most important medical journal of the day, because the latter had accused him in print of incompetence in an operation for the removal of a bladder stone, resulting in the death of the patient. The operation – in the era before anaesthetics – had lasted for one hour, instead of the few minutes that it should have done, and which was as much as any person could be expected to endure. The patient, not surprisingly, died in the most terrible agony imaginable.

The trial for libel was a *cause célèbre*; the police had difficulty in controlling the crowds that wanted to attend. Wakley defended himself, and though technically he lost the trial, in reality he won, only one penny in damages being awarded against him. Cooper's reputation was severely damaged.[5]

Dickson's reputation, as that of the most consistent and ferocious medical opponent of blood-letting, was not improved by the publication of the pamphlet in which he did not hesitate to name names, in a manner no doubt regarded by the rest of the profession as disloyal. He had first become an opponent of blood-letting in India where he was a young army surgeon, and where he carried out blood-letting as the then-orthodox treatment required in cases of typhoid, cholera and malaria. He noticed that most of his patients died, either despite or because of the treatment, and from then on he carried on a relentless campaign against it, suggesting (unusually for the time) a controlled trial against other, less drastic methods of treatment. By the end of his life, in 1869, blood-letting – after a career centuries and even millennia long – had become old-fashioned, never to be revived.[6] But Dickson reaped no benefit, not even gratitude, for having been right: he was the victim of the natural history of widespread but obvious error. By the time that error is exposed as such, everyone claims never to have believed it anyway, to have always known that it was error; and Dickson, in so far as he was right all along, was held to have been right for the wrong reasons. His obituary in the *Medical Times and Gazette* characterised him as a man of only 'moderate ability' who had 'a talent for abuse which he exercised to an unlimited extent.'[7] It is surely very galling when men of moderate ability are able to see what many far more brilliant men have not seen for hundreds or thousands of years.

Thomas Hodge, by contrast with Edward Drummond, was not so much actively killed by treatment as not saved when he need not have died. By the time Dr Dickson arrived, Hodge (who had cried out 'I am stabbed!' rather than '*Je suis stabbé!*, as had

Le Cronier) was already dead – or, in the words of the inquest,
'had ceased to live.' But at the trial, several doctors called by the
defence testified that if only pressure had been applied properly to
the wound and the severed artery, the victim would have survived.
This was important, because it gave the impression that John
Noon had not inflicted an inevitably fatal wound upon Thomas
Hodge, with the implication that he had not really intended, or
committed, murder.

Strictly speaking, the evidence given by the doctors was
irrelevant. If a man dies as a result of a serious wound deliberately
inflicted by someone else, the crime is murder, even if the medical
treatment the victim received after the wound was sub-optimal and
even if the intention was only seriously to injure, not to kill. Thus
Noon was guilty of murder, unless it was held that he was seriously
provoked (though, according to the evidence, he had done most
of the provoking). But to have passed the death penalty on a man
whose victim might have been saved by a little firm pressure on the
wound would no doubt have been repellent to people who clearly
had doubts about the justification of that penalty. Noon's action
was reprehensible, but it was not sufficiently *evil* to overcome the
qualms that many people had.

Of the three victims of homicide in Jersey between December
1845 and February 1846, two would probably have survived
nowadays. Noon would have been saved by a passer-by with
first aid training; Le Cronier by surgery. This factor – improved
medical care of the injured – is often forgotten when comparisons
are made between the murder rates of different historical epochs.
Recent American research suggested that, if the same medical
and surgical techniques were employed today as were employed
in 1960, the number of homicides now would be five times higher
than it is. If the estimate is correct, and if figures are applicable
in Britain, where the actual homicide rate has doubled in the
intervening period, it would mean that the homicidal attack rate
has increased ten times since 1960. And it should be remembered

that, from the point of view of advance in surgical technique, the difference between 1845-6 and 1960 was even greater than that between 1960 and 2010.

Against this must be set the possibility that, in a society in which there is a very high death rate from natural causes, and pathological investigation is only rudimentary, murder would be easier to disguise as death from natural cause. Where death is ever-present, and often comes in waves, no death is entirely unexpected. In 1960, Dr John Havard (later president of the British Medical Association) published a book titled *The Detection of Secret Homicide*. He wrote:

> The inflated publicity accorded to murders where travelling trunks, acid baths, lime burials, and other irregular methods of disposal are employed, may lead us to overlook the fact that these methods are rarely used by the resourceful murderer. The number of cases in which the discovery that the body of a murdered person has been disposed of as a natural death has only been made as a result of investigation into a later and recognised murder, allow us to assume that many murderers must be entirely successful in avoiding detection.[8]

The career, if that is quite the word for it, of Dr Harold Shipman, bears this out. But it also shows that in the modern world, hidden homicide is just as possible as it was in Victorian times. While in Victorian times the theoretical likelihood of the recognition of homicide was perhaps less than it is now, the modern murderer has more means at his disposal to bring about the death of his victim (an extension of consumer choice). And the constant decline in the proportion of post mortem examinations since 1960 has probably emboldened those inclined secretly to murder.

XV

The acquittal of Madame Le Gendre of the charge of murder, in favour of the lesser charge of *homicide voluntaire*, caused stupefaction on the island, and indeed gave rise, briefly, to unrest. There were some disturbances – 'in which the knife played its part' – in the wake of the verdict. 'It is to be hoped,' said the *Chronique*, 'that the Royal Court will punish these individuals severely, as an example to others, and return to our island that calm and tranquillity that these events have interrupted.'[1]

It is surely odd, though typically human, that some of those outraged by the failure of a court to punish severely enough the perpetrator of an isolated act of violence should resort themselves in protest to violence of a similar kind. In our own day we have seen men and women scream and shout abuse in the street as an alleged paedophile is brought to court in a police van, with their own terrified small children in tow.

The verdict and the case in general gave rise to strong and long-lasting polemics. Among the matters discussed was the justification and efficacy or otherwise of the death penalty in general; the necessity or otherwise for a professional police force in Jersey; and the effect upon the conduct of Madame Le Gendre of the agitation in the newspapers (principally *L'Impartial*) against the then system of policing on the island.

The verdict was widely regarded as indefensible and even illegal. It flew in the face of the evidence, and everyone in the court was astonished: if anyone was ever guilty of murder, Madame Le Gendre was. It was revealed that, originally, 21 of the 24 members of the *Grande Enquête* had voted for murder, enough to convict; but then two changed their minds, and voted for voluntary homicide. What could explain their sudden *volte face*?

It was thought that they had originally planned to vote for murder but with an appeal for clemency. However, the court

117

would not have had to listen to that appeal, indeed would have had *not* to listen to it, and instead would have had to pass the mandatory sentence of death. Under the law of the time, only the Secretary for the Home Department, Sir James Graham, could have acted upon it, and it was by no means certain that he would have done so.

If members of the jury acquitted because of opposition to the death penalty, they were not keeping to their oath as jurymen. According to that oath, they swore to render a verdict 'in which you believe,' and that 'you will render… without favour or partiality, as you would answer before God.' There is no mention in the oath of altering a verdict because of disapproval of the punishment it would bring the guilty.

The suspected failure of the jurymen to render a true verdict outraged the *Chronique*.[2] If the jurymen had objected to the death penalty they could, presumably, have made their views known beforehand, and thus be excused jury service. But they might well have thought it morally more important or imperative to prevent an execution than to abide by an oath. Immanuel Kant's notion that there is a categorical imperative always to speak the truth, even to the extent that one had a duty to point a murderer in the direction of his victim if he asks where the victim is, has not found many adherents; and there was plenty of precedent in British legal history for the conduct of the jurors in the Le Gendre case. It is well-known that the Bloody Code, which made so many crimes capital, was repealed not so much out of consideration for the criminals who were subject to its provisions, but because juries refused to convict them and thereby allowed them to get away scot-free. Property was therefore unprotected by this theoretical severity; and Parliament received many petitions for a relaxation in the law: In 1819, bankers wrote to Parliament:

> Your petitioners find by experience that the infliction of death, or even the possibility of the

118

infliction of death, prevents the prosecution, conviction and punishment of the criminal, and thus endangers the property which it is intended to protect.[3]

This was because juries refused to convict; and the relaxation of the Bloody Code (leaving murder, treason, piracy and arson in her Majesty's shipyards the only capital offences by the time of Madame le Gendre's offence) was more recent in 1846 than is the abolition of the death penalty, or even the decimalisation of our currency, to us.

The Reverend Clement Perrot was editor of *The Jersey Herald* between 1845 and 1847, two years before his death. He had long been a widower; his wife, Susanna Maria Sharp, who was the founder of Sunday schools in Jersey, died one of the most absurd deaths of which I have ever heard. In 1819, she fell off the stage while giving out Sunday school prizes, and succumbed to her injuries.

Although practically no copies of the Reverend Perrot's newspaper survive, by chance a series of the columns that he wrote for the newspaper he edited survive in bound form in the Lord Coutanche Library of the *Société Jersiaise*. He gave himself the pseudonym of Caesariensis, the name of Jersey being believed to be etymologically derived from Caesar. Under the title *A Strange Verdict!!!* (the three exclamation marks being a genuine testimony to its strangeness, for unlike S. T. Coleridge, say, the Reverend Perrot was not given to peppering his prose with idle punctuation mark to indicate to the reader just how deeply he felt), the editor distinguishes clearly between the question of the death penalty and that of Madame Le Gendre's guilt:

However much we may condemn the severity of the law and pity both judge and jury placed under the stern necessity of declaring its awards, and the facts on which they depend, we cannot conceal from ourselves that their duty is so plain and distinct, that it leaves no room for their exercise of their judgment as to the proportion between the crime and the punishment. The judge has naught to do but with the letter of the law, and the jury has no concern but with the truth or falsehood adduced in support of the accusation.[4]

It would be quite wrong to conclude from this that the Reverend Perrot was a kind of ecclesiastical Madame Defarge, who waited impatiently for the death penalty to be passed so that he could moralise at the foot of the scaffold. On the contrary, he began his article with what sounds uncommonly like a condemnation of that very penalty:

He has made himself little acquainted with human nature, and has been little observant of the violence of human passions once set free from the restraints of humanity and the enactments of acknowledged justice, who feels astonishment at the wholesale massacres, at the untold hecatombs of victims immolated to the demon of war. Fearful as is the din of battle, the cries of the dying, the sighs of widows and orphans, and all the untold evils attendant on the deadly conflict of hostile armies; – fearful as we are of all these, there is something more appalling in the sanguinary code of many a nation which dooms to death, with little more mercy than the laws of Draco, almost every offender. Here death is not the infuriated infliction of maddened passions, but the cool, tranquil, and deliberate resolve of philosophers and lawgivers.[5]

But the Reverend Perrot was not a mushy sentimentalist, and was clearly an intelligent man. He draws a distinction that is all too often lost between justice and mercy, the two *desiderata* pulling in different directions (indeed, there would hardly be a need for mercy if justice were not sometimes hard in its dictates):

> Do we then [he asks] regret that a miserable female has escaped the extreme penalty of the law? Far from us be the thought! But we do regret most deeply that she has escaped, not by the exercise of mercy, but under the semblance of justice.[6]

Though the Reverend Perrot is not bloodthirsty, and does not want Madame Le Gendre executed in public or at all, he is a believer in the death penalty, not in every case of a given category of crime, but as a possibility hovering in the background, as it were, giving pause to every potential evil-doer. He continues:

> We would have had her life spared without endangering that of every police officer on the island. This we mean; that whatever removes a salutary restraint is an encouragement to crime, and that the fear of the gallows is such a restraint. We know that whatever discourages and weakens the exercise of the executive power proportionately endangers the peace and security of society. If the restless and disorderly are emboldened to resist, and even to ill-treat those charged with the repression of their evil deeds, who can fairly condemn those continually exposed to their violence, if, from regard to their personal safety, they hesitate in exposing themselves to the danger of insult, ill-treatment and perhaps death.[7]

Things turned out, according to him, just as he feared. A short time later he wrote:

> The infamous, and either ignorant or depraved –
> it *must* have been one or the other – verdict in the
> case of Le Gendre, is filling the island with the most
> desperate crimes.[8]
>
> Within the last few weeks various savage attacks
> with *the knife* have been made on several persons
> and the police, from some cause or other, are still
> the objects of the threats and vengeance of those
> ruffians. The idea that no crime, however great,
> will in this island be punished by death, is now
> affording to the public a pretty good illustration
> of the disastrous consequences which would result
> from the total abolition of that punishment, and the
> perfect impossibility of controlling the evil deeds of
> desperate men by such bugbears as imprisonment
> or transportation.

The matter is more difficult than the Reverend Perrot supposes, of course. The fact that event *B* follows hard upon event *A* does not go to prove that event *B* was *caused* by event *A*. This is a typical journalist's fallacy, and I have committed it myself in my eagerness to comment – for money – upon the emblematic significance of some unusual (and, of course, always terrible or horrible) episode.

There is, of course, the well-known *Werther* effect which, if it exists at all, is short-lived. It is named for Goethe's novel, *The Sorrows of Young Werther*, in which the hero killed himself for unrequited love. It was immensely popular all over Europe when it was published (though it is all but unreadable now), and it is said that many a young man killed himself at the end of the 18th century in imitation of it. Nowadays, if a young and attractive

person is shown on television committing suicide, there is a rash
of imitative suicides, the victims perhaps themselves victims of
faulty reasoning:

> Personage A was fascinating, and committed
> suicide.
> I commit suicide, therefore I must be fascinating.

The problem with deciding whether the Werther effect is real
is statistical. Clusters of unusual or rare events do occur, indeed
must occur. For example, I was once asked to investigate a spate
of murders carried out by psychiatric patients in the same area.
At first sight, they were connected in some way or other because
such a spate or cluster was most unusual and was unlikely to have
occurred by chance; but a professional statistician established
that it might well have occurred by chance, because somewhere
in the country clusters of rare events that appear not to have
occurred by chance *must* sometimes occur by chance. This is so
for purely mathematical reasons, almost by definition as it were;
and, although in this instance the investigation did reveal an
abysmally low standard of care, it could not be established on the
evidence that the murders (except in one case) took place *because*
of the abysmal standard of care. Most abysmal care of psychiatric
patients, after all, does not end in murder, which remains a rare
event.

The Reverend Perrot was not aware of these complexities;
even the most intellectually sophisticated and scrupulous person
is aware of them only intermittently and by effort of will. Few
(and boring) are those who confine their opinions to statements for
which there is the strictest evidence. I doubt whether anyone at the
time replied to the good Reverend that his article did not present,
let alone constitute, any evidence whatsoever that the number of
knife attacks in Jersey had increased after the Le Gendre verdict,
to say nothing of the question as to whether a single verdict

such as the one in her case could have given the impression that the death penalty was abolished, when only very shortly before Thomas Nicolle had been sentenced to death (his reprieve having been far from a foregone conclusion).

What evidence might one seek to establish on a firmer basis than mere reactive outrage, such as that of Reverend Perrot, that the death penalty acts as a deterrent to potential evil-doers, and to demonstrate 'the disastrous consequences which would result from the total abolition of that punishment'? This has puzzled and taxed the minds of both abolitionists and those (a minority among intellectuals, but often a substantial majority among the general population) who wanted to retain it.

One method, of course, is to compare the homicide rates of jurisdictions that employ and do not employ the death penalty. But this is not very satisfactory because jurisdictions are likely to differ in far more than the employment or non-employment of that penalty, for example in their general culture, history, consumption of alcohol, age structure and so forth. More satisfactory, perhaps, would be the study of a single jurisdiction in which the death penalty was abolished, but even this method would have to be approached with care. It is often stated, for example, that prohibition of alcohol in the United States was a failure in its aims, because the murder rate went up while it was in force. This is true; the murder rate *did* go up; but what is less often pointed out is that the murder rate in the United States went up even more, proportionately, in the years before Prohibition. Here, then, is a possible example of precisely the fallacy of *post hoc ergo propter hoc* to which the Reverend Perrot fell victim in the article quoted above: the murder rate went up during Prohibition, therefore it went up *because* of Prohibition. And, by analogy, one would have to be cautious in concluding that, if the homicide rate increased after the abolition of the death penalty, it increased *because* of the abolition of the death penalty.

There are other complications. It is possible that the abolition would have a delayed, and not an immediate, effect. For example, I grew up taking the existence of the death penalty more or less for granted: when a man was found guilty of murder he was automatically sentenced to death, even if the sentence was actually carried out in only a small proportion of the cases in which the sentence was passed. Thus I spent my formative years absorbing the impression (among many others, of course) that you might be hanged for killing someone; such an impression, once absorbed, was likely to have a lasting, if subliminal, effect on me and my outlook. It would be quite otherwise with someone growing up when there was no possibility of capital punishment because it had been abolished.[9]

There is, however, one other method that might be employed. It is a truism that the murder rate will never be reduced to zero, that the mark of Cain is forever imprinted upon mankind, and that the war against murder is never won in the sense of a final victory over it having been achieved. In any society there will be an irreducible minimum of murder, though it is not easy to say what this minimum would be. This means, in effect, that there are some murders that would not be prevented or deterred by the prospect of any punishment whatsoever, the impulse to kill overwhelming all other considerations and rendering them nugatory.

In the year in which the *Murder (Abolition of Death Penalty) Bill* was passed, 1965, the distinguished psychiatrist and criminologist, Donald West, published a short and lucid book called *Murder Followed by Suicide*.[10] This, as the title suggests, was a study of the phenomenon of murder followed by the suicide of the murderer. Interestingly, this type of murder accounted in England and Wales for about a third of murders known to the police, and had done so for many years, since the 1920s at least. Professor West studied the characteristics of these murders, their victims and their perpetrators, and compared them with 'ordinary' murders.

Several characteristics emerged from this comparison, as one might have expected. Murderers who went on to kill themselves were usually less criminally-inclined than other murderers; far fewer of them had criminal records, they were often respectable, of higher social class with better employment histories. Their motive was usually the tragic resolution of a terrible and painful dilemma, whether that dilemma existed in reality or was a figment of their diseased imagination. For example, a middle-aged bachelor of regular habits and with no criminal record, who lived with his aged and incapacitated mother, had to go into hospital for an operation on cancer; fearing that his mother would not be able to cope without him, either temporarily or permanently (in the event of his own death), he killed her and then killed himself. Or again, a depressed but otherwise doting father came to believe delusionally that he has passed on incurable venereal disease to his wife and children, and killed them all and then himself to avoid the otherwise unavoidable suffering that he had inflicted upon them. A mother, believing that she had passed on a horrible and incurable disease to her children, killed them from a misplaced sense of love for them.

Rather as suicide bombers are not easy to deter by threats, so this type of murderer is unlikely to take the death penalty (or any other penalty) into account in deciding to act as he does. Such murderers do not have what one might call normal criminal intentions – an inheritance, for example, or the furtherance of a robbery or burglary – in their minds when they kill. Their emotional state is such as to drive all normal prudential considerations from their minds.

Now if, after the abolition of the death penalty, the previously stable proportion of murders followed by suicide declined – that is to say, other types of murder increased in number and proportion to the whole, while the absolute number of murder followed by suicide remained stable – as a result of an increase in the total number of murders, this would be at least *prima facie* evidence for the deterrent effect of the death penalty, for those other types of murder would be more susceptible to deterrence and normal prudential considerations, such as the desire to avoid being hanged.[11]

For many years, those who committed homicide were, like Gaul, divided into three: those who killed themselves immediately or very soon afterwards, those who were found to be insane or (after the Homicide Act came into force in 1957) of diminished responsibility and therefore guilty 'only' of manslaughter, and those held to be fully responsible for their acts. These proportions were stable for a long time; if, therefore, they changed after the abolition of the death penalty, such that a larger proportion of perpetrators were held fully responsible for their acts, it would suggest that the death penalty had indeed acted as a deterrent.[12]

Even this evidence, however, would be open to other interpretations. For example, Professor West found that murder-suicide was relatively common among women (or, more accurately, a much larger proportion of perpetrators of murder-suicide were women than of other types of homicide). In the vast majority of cases, they killed their children as well as themselves, and the method that they used in 30 out of 36 cases was poisoning by coal gas. Since the switch to natural gas, which is not poisonous, such a non-violent method – which Professor West calls 'passive' – is no longer available. Hence a decline in the *relative* rate of murder-suicide might reflect a change in the gas supply rather than in the inclination to murder, and hence the deterrent effect of the death penalty might be overestimated.[13]

Similarly, the number of perpetrators of homicide found not fully responsible for their acts might be susceptible (in either direction) to changes in diagnostic and legal fashion: that is to say, medical examiners might be more (or less) likely to find, and courts to accept, exculpatory explanations of murderous acts. Few can doubt that there has been a tendency, since Professor West wrote his book, for explanation to take the sting from blame. For example, I recently read in a medical report on a woman who had stabbed a man to death, as far as I could tell without the presence of many mitigating factors, that, 'Initially she felt very guilty, but after counselling accepted that she was the victim of circumstances.' A *Zeitgeist* in which such a thing could be written not as satire but seriously, as evidence of increased insight into her actions by the perpetrator of a cold-blooded murder, is one in which every effort will be made to exculpate almost anyone of anything. Therefore, the proportion of perpetrators found to be suffering from some exculpatory or mitigating psychological condition might very well have risen by comparison with what it would have been if the same criteria were used as nearly half a century ago. And if Madame Le Gendre were to have stabbed M. *le Centenier* Le Cronier now, no doubt some counsellor, having read in Norman Mailer's essay *The White Negro* that 'it takes faith in the creative possibilities of the human being to envisage acts of violence as the catharsis which prepares growth,'[14] would persuade her that her slaying of the *centenier* was the means by which her butterfly could emerge from her chrysalis.

Caveats and reservations notwithstanding, I suspect that the Reverend Perrot's belief that the death penalty was a deterrent was correct overall, even if he was mistaken about the effect of its non-application in Madame Le Gendre's case. That, as we have seen, is not quite the same as justifying the death penalty altogether. A penalty is not necessarily justified because it is effective, as those who object to the amputation of thieves' hands know.

XVI

A further argument against the death penalty was deployed in the correspondence columns of the *Constitutionnel* soon after the verdict in the Le Gendre trial: what might be called the there-but-for-the-Grace-of-God-go-we-all argument.

Most of the correspondents to the newspapers used pseudonyms, such as *Pere de famille, Demosthenes, Veritas, Vale, Scrutator* or, in this case, *Castigator* (an odd choice in view of what he had to say, as it is not clear whom he is castigating). And why the correspondents resorted to pseudonyms I cannot tell; perhaps in a small and isolated community such as that of Jersey, where emotions could easily run high, differences of opinion between private individuals were best kept abstract and impersonal. It was all right for editors to be beaten in the street – it was a hazard of the job, in fact – but not for people who were private figures. Presumably most of the correspondents to the newspapers were of the upper echelons of society, and it would have been a poor example to the lower if they had set about beating one another in the street for something that they had written.

Castigator wrote:[1]

> Sir,
>
> Since the day when the verdict of the *Grande Enquête* was given in the trial of the woman Le Gendre, the pages of the police faction have done nothing but denounce the members of the jury who acquitted that unfortunate of the crime of murder; as if those gentlemen who expressed their opinion according to the oath that they took hadn't a right to their own opinion.
>
> In truth, the poor people who write those wretched miserable sheets must have a great thirst

129

for blood so to regret that a spectacle, both hideous and shocking to morality, should not take place on *Mont-patibulaire.*[3]

But have those writers reflected that one day the principles that they cite in favour of the death penalty might be fatal to themselves, or to theirs? For where is the man who can say that he will never strike a blow? Or who can flatter himself that his children, or his children's children, will never be placed, because of what they have done, even by accident, under the avenging word of justice? He does not exist. The man who is today surrounded by the esteem of his fellow-citizens can tomorrow become a criminal...

Castigator's is a lamentable argument, and *Castigator* himself also fits admirably Oscar Wilde's definition of a sentimentalist as 'one who desires to have the luxury of an emotion without paying for it.'

Castigator omits to mention that Madame Le Gendre did not merely 'strike a blow.' On the contrary, she announced her murderous intention beforehand; had a knife sharpened the very morning that she used it; she laid it by her in an unaccustomed place convenient for use; and then stabbed without genuine provocation. She would also have stabbed someone else if she had been able, and threatened to stab anyone who came to her house. This is not something that 'anyone' might do; it is not a sudden loss of control because of an access of emotion. So determined is *Castigator* to show his superior compassion and understanding that he fails to fix his mind on the actual details of the case.

But even if stabbing George Le Cronier was something that anyone *might* do, the law has to take notice of what people actually *have* done; it is not its function to speculate as to what they *might* do, for then it would make almost as much sense to place people under preventive detention in case they committed murder as to fail to punish murderers because anyone might have been a murderer.[4] And in fact, *Castigator*'s argument against the death penalty, if valid, would be equally valid against any punishment whatsoever, for example transportation for life (to which Madame Le Gendre was sentenced). For what parent, say, would want his child removed to the other side of the world, with scant likelihood that he would ever see him again this side of Paradise? Or, indeed, would want him punished in any way whatsoever?

No one, I trust, would wish the punishment of criminals to be determined by their victims or (in the case of murder) their victims' relatives. One of the reasons that we have a system of justice, after all, is to control the natural, primitive and almost universal thirst for vengeance that so easily results in vendetta. But there is no reason, either, to hand over punishment to the relatives of the punished. If justice must be tempered by mercy, so mercy must be tempered by justice. There might be arguments against the death penalty, but *Castigator*'s — that we might any of us end up on the scaffold — is not one of them.[5]

It is worth speculating a little about *Castigator*'s psychology. Why did he make such an exhibition, if I may so put it, of his sympathy for Madame Le Gendre? There were, after all, many arguments against the public execution of murderers other than that the murderer is not so very different from the rest of us.[6]

Castigator might with justice have said, 'Thank goodness the jury found Le Gendre guilty of manslaughter and not murder, thereby sparing us the abhorrent spectacle of a public execution; indeed, that is the probable reason for its verdict. It is time public executions were abolished.' But he went much further. Like the schoolboy who thinks that his excuse for not doing his homework is much stronger if the ink spilt on it *and* the dog ate it *and* it flew out of the window *and* it burnt in the fire, *Castigator* thinks his case is stronger if he dissolves the distinction between murderers and non-murderers. By doing so, he is showing that he is superior in sensibility to those vulgar souls – the great majority, apparently – who were appalled by the murder of George Le Cronier, whose reaction was thoughtless, immediate, and primitive.

The desire to distinguish oneself morally from the majority, as a sign *ipso facto* of superior understanding and generosity of spirit, probably begins in Victorian times. The impulse to forgive others not for what they have done to oneself, but for what they have done to third parties, in order to prove one's freedom from vulgar prejudice, is very much with us, as exemplified by the late Lord Packenham, who noisily absolved many criminals of their guilt – provided they were high-profile enough.

XVII

The Reverend Perrot drew attention to the role of the press in provoking Madame Le Gendre to murder:

> They ['the whole community of desperate characters that infest Jersey's shores'] are stimulated in this morbid excitement by an infamous and degraded press.[1]

As far as I can tell, 'an infamous and degraded press' is a euphemism for *Le Constitutionnel* and the *Jersey and Guernsey News*, the former being the only newspaper that I have been able to find that criticised, and criticised relentlessly, the then system of policing in Jersey. The surviving journals of the period are few; but since Abraham Jones Le Cras edited the *Jersey and Guernsey News*, and was a ferocious opponent of the system of policing as well as the whole of Jersey's criminal justice system, it is probably that the Reverend Perrot considered his newspaper (practically no examples of which survive) to be part of 'the infamous and degraded press.' Certainly, the Reverend was no admirer of Mr Le Cras; for when a Royal Commission was appointed to look into the criminal law of Jersey, he wrote that the enquiry was 'evidently nothing more than a bone thrown to a hungry animal (who shall be nameless) to keep him quiet, and prevent him barking too often at what he does not understand.'[2]

The hungry animal who barked at what, allegedly, he did not understand could only have been Abraham Jones Le Cras, author of tracts against the supposedly immemorial independence of Jersey.

In the wake of the murder of Le Cronier, the two newspapers which happily still exist in almost complete runs for 1845 and 1846, *Le Chronique de Jersey* and *Le Constitutionnel*, engaged on a long and bitter war of words, a war of accusation, recrimination, refutation and counter-accusation; as in love and war, all was fair in this war of words.

The ideological position of the two newspapers was somewhat contradictory. In Jersey in the 19th century there were two political parties, as they were called, the Laurel and the Rose. They were called parties, but they were informal factions rather than formally constituted political parties with membership, subscriptions, etc.

The Laurel party had its support in rural areas, principally among the traditional *patois*-speaking farmers. It was therefore conservative in outlook.

The Rose party was supported by the ever-more numerous English immigrants to the island, by the English tradesmen who catered to their needs, and by the French-speaking population of St Helier that was engaged in commerce. It was more liberal in outlook, modernising, Anglophile and anglicising, and economistic.[3]

The *Chronique de Jersey* was generally regarded as the mouthpiece of the Rose party or faction, *Le Constitutionnel* as that of the Laurel.

This being so, the *Chronique* should have attacked the police system, wanting it to be replaced by a system similar to that of the newly-established Metropolitan Police, while *Le Constitutionnel* should have argued for the maintenance of the *status quo*. In fact, it was precisely the opposite; the *Chronique* implied that everything was already for the best and nothing needed changing, while *Le Constitutionnel* argued that the police were lazy, ineffective, corrupt and failing utterly in their duty to protect the public. Indeed, it would hardly be too much to say that it was obsessed by this subject.

Le Constitutionnel, the famous *Journal du bien public*, was edited by another stormy petrel of Jersey journalism, Jean Nicolas René de la Croix, who lived between 1796 and 1869. His career was very varied; he had been in turn a tailor, farmer, schoolmaster, editor, author, musician, sacristan, second-hand dealer and then once more editor.[4] According to *A Biographical Dictionary of Jersey*, '(t)wo things wrecked his influence, the vileness of the personal abuse in which he indulged, and the fact that he was ready to write for whichever side paid him best.'

The *Dictionary* says that, for a time, he edited newspapers for both principal parties, the Rose and the Laurel. 'The *Chronique* had proof that he had also been secretly editing the *Gazette*, and inserting articles in one paper, which he answered in the other.'[5]

He was dismissed for a time from the editorship of *Le Constitutionnel*, but talented editors were not very many in Jersey (nor, perhaps, anywhere else), and before long he was taken back, like – nowadays – a British government minister who resigns temporarily because of some impropriety, financial or sexual.

At any rate, by the time the controversy over the Le Gendre murder broke out, Jean Nicolas René De La Croix seems to have developed fixed opinions, approaching monomania, that it is difficult to believe that he did not sincerely hold. Neither his previous duplicity nor his later fixity of purpose seems to have brought him much in the way of wealth or worldly reward, however: when a man who believed himself to have been traduced in his pages went to Le Croix's house, in a poor neighbourhood of St Helier, with the intention of throwing a brick through his window, he came away with the brick still in his hand because none of the windows of the house was glazed, the editor being too poor to glaze them – unless, of course, his windows were regularly put out by angry readers.

So poor was he, in fact, that he needed another string to his bow, that of *brocanteur*, or dealer in junk and items of small value. He was also a pawnbroker. As a consequence, the editor of the *Chronique* sometimes referred to him in the controversy between the newspapers as *l'éditeur-brocanteur*. Because the editor of the *Chronique* believed (wrongly) that De La Croix had attended a Jesuit school, he also called him the Editor-Jesuit. As it happens, the editor of the *Chronique* had a satisfactory explanation (that is to say, an explanation that satisfied *him*) as to why the editor-junk-dealer-Jesuit so hated the police of Jersey as they were then constituted. The hostility between the newspapers about this matter existed even before Madame Le Gendre took to the knife. In the *Chronique* for Wednesday, 4 February, 1846, all is explained:

> One reads in *Le Constitutionnel* for last Saturday the following paragraph:
>
> 'Although one believed that the cruel punishment of flogging had been abolished in the Army, a certain Brown, a soldier in the garrison on this island of the 81st Regiment, received a hundred strokes of the strap on Thursday last, as a punishment for theft, and in consequence of a judgment against him by a Court Martial.'
>
> It seems that the Editor of *Le Constitutionnel* deplores that this punishment still exists in the Army. Ah! the excellent man! And yet it is this same man who has vowed a mortal hatred of the police of St Helier, and who insults it every week[6], because M. *le Centenier* Chevalier arrested him for having whipped, not his horse, but his wife... It was because this precious instrument was taken from him by M. *le Centenier* Chevalier... Furthermore, he did not punish his wife after a Court Martial; oh no, he punished her without any judgment, and he was at the same time husband, judge, jury and executioner!
>
> It is this degraded man that the owners of *Le Constitutionnel* – the party of *Gentlemen* – employ to insult their Opponents and the Assembly of the Parish of St Helier, whom he reproaches for having *brutally* refused to admit some electors...[7]

> The word is not well-chosen: if this refusal had
> been unjustified, there would have been *injustice*,
> not *brutality*. This word applies only to a husband
> who beats his wife with a whip. Let the editor of *Le
> Constitutionnel* learn the real meaning of words, and
> to keep the word *brutal* for himself.

Not surprisingly, perhaps, M. De La Croix did not let this go
unanswered. Strictly speaking, the character of a man making
an argument does not affect the validity of that argument, but
it is only human – ineradicably human – to be interested in the
conduct of a man who argues against what you believe.[8] M. De La
Croix answered in his next edition:[9]

> We will not here reveal why [*Centenier* Chevalier]
> left his wife to go on a voyage to Plymouth with
> someone else. Who invited him thus to take himself
> off? For us the secret – For posterity to know.[10]

This was not exactly a forensic refutation of the charge of
having beaten his wife, but it no doubt served as a distraction from
that charge. De La Croix had, after all, threatened to write, and
claimed actually to be writing, *The Black Book of Jersey*, in which
such information about every prominent person on the island
would be revealed to the world. The *Biographical Dictionary* tells
us that it is fortunate that this book never saw the light of day – a
judgment with which it would no doubt be very wrong, indeed
frivolous, of me to disagree.

The Editor-Jesuit did not confine his threat of revelations to
come to M. *le Centenier* Chevalier, but went further up the hierarchy,
to the *Connétable* of St Helier himself, M. le Sueur:

> Let him know, by the way, that a precious manuscript
> has fallen into our hands, written in the form of a

diary by one of the members of his family, rich in details: we will know how to use it when the time is right. For the rest, we thank the *Chronique* for having re-awakened our old memories. We can assure it that its friends will not be the losers by it.

Another article in *Le Constitutionnel* is slightly more to the point, but does not actually go so far as to deny that he hit his wife and had been arrested for it:

The *Chronique* of last Wednesday claimed that the police of St Helier is perfect and beyond the reproach of brutality.

Accuse us of *injustice*, if you like, it said, but not of *brutality*; for the difference is great. We agree, but we do not know how to, nor can we, make the distinction between these two amiable qualities where the police are concerned. They both apply to them equally. If when a person raises his voice to protest against injustice, his mouth is shut by shouts and jeers – when he is spoken to grossly and insolently, told that that is all he deserves, that he owes rent, and old confidential conversations are dragged up with the aim of humiliating him; all this is deemed politeness (or good manners)...

When you are threatened with being thrown out, when about twenty confederates dance around him and shout in chorus to drown out the voice of the protester, there is neither injustice or brutality according to the vocabulary of certain people. And if it is necessary to give more recent proof, we ask if the law permits a Police officer, of whatever rank, to hit a prisoner? Has he the right to slap anyone's face? – No. Yet has that not happened this week?

– Yes. We abstain for the moment from naming names; but if necessary we will quote them, and other *kindnesses* of this type...

The *Chronique*, unsurprisingly, did not take this lying down either. In its following edition[11], it editorialised:

Outraged by the crude attacks that *Le Constitutionnel* pours every day[12] on the public servants whom it cannot accuse of any other crime than that of zealously fulfilling the onerous positions that they fill, we, in our edition of last Wednesday, had made known the *cause* of the inveterate hatred that the editor of this rabble-rousing journal has vowed against these public servants; here now is how this editor replies:

They do not know the man they're dealing with, the impudent rogues! Let them know, then, these coarse creatures, ephemeral flies, or rather *strange* wasps, that the Editor of the *Constitutionnel* is also the author of *La Ville de Saint-Hélier* [The Town of St Helier]!!! and that he holds in his hands the future destiny of the madmen who dare today to provoke him!!! TO EVERYONE HIS TURN. TO THE ALL-POWERFUL – ETERNITY. TO THE FUTURE HISTORIAN OF JERSEY – POSTERITY!!!!!!!!!!!!

We did not know with what man we had to deal: we thought that he was an ignoble and contemptible being, whose sole talent was hatred, whose sole *métier* was calumny; we did not think we had to deal with a madman... it is now that we realise it for the first time. Self-love, stupid vanity has so turned the head of this poor imbecile, that he sets up a parallel between the Divinity and himself. TO EACH HIS TURN, he writes, and wants to give way to the ALL-POWERFUL, but then he has to share with God: AU TOUT-PUISSANT L'ÉTERNITÉ A JEAN LA CROIX, LA POSTERITÉ And soon, no doubt, altars!!! [to himself]... As for us, we will grant him the madman's bells – for no one but a madman would dare to write such sentences!!!

Furthermore, he is a madman as ignorant as he is conceited: because he has written a miserable pamphlet, he believes himself to be a great man who does not even know that he does not know the language in which he writes: thus, he uses *bizarrure*, a word that exists in no language, instead of *bizarrerie*. His insipid pamphlet is written in a similar style; author and pamphlet alike suit only humble houses... It is there that posterity awaits them.

I do not think that anyone would deny that Jean De la Croix's reply to the revelation that he had beaten his wife and had been arrested for it was intemperate, beside the point, blackmailing in tone and probably in part the product of a guilty conscience. And yet the *Chronique*'s reply to his reply also has unpleasant aspects, for example that of snobbery. How dare a man so humble as once to have been a tailor presume to write! How could such a man's *pamphlet*, as the *Chronique* called his volume of 250 closely-printed pages, and which was more considerable than anything the editor of the *Chronique* ever wrote, be anything other than miserable? Because de la Croix makes one mistake, he is called an ignoramus[13], a man so ignorant that he does not know that he's ignorant. In fact, the man's book, and his subsequent books, are regarded by historians of Jersey as serious contributions to history, the author having immersed himself in the primary documents of previous eras. And his so-called miserable pamphlet is actually not without genuine moral passion:

Let us try to show, in a few words, the worthlessness and inefficacy of the institutions that rule us. We have in this country which is so beautiful, so happily endowed by nature – apart from the political and moral influence of England, a political influence that dominates us by a constant immigration of people of doubtful morals for whom the island serves as an asylum and refuge – three political bodies, namely the States[14], the Royal Court and the Police.

Each of these bodies has for its mission the repression of the vices of society and to work for the general and private good; but none of them, it is painful to have to admit, bother to find the causes of the vices, much less the remedies.

There follows a passionate peroration worthy of Karl Marx when the latter condemns the supposed hypocrisy of the moralising bourgeoisie (Marx, incidentally, used quite often to holiday on Jersey, and was himself no mean hypocrite when it came to money):

The poor are imprisoned to hide beggary from view; they are consigned to hospital where, if they were only among their companions in misfortune, they would be happy; but no; they are mixed with *filles publiques*, people without morals, law or religion,[15] Poverty is treated on the same footing as crime: it is coupled with vice. Drunkenness [in Jersey] is at its apogee, and never did a more demoralising or hideous social sore so disfigure a society. What do they do to repress it? On the one hand they multiply the taverns, on the other they pretend by legal restrictions to modify the rules that govern them![16]

Plus ca change! In the small, rural, market town in England in which I live, a licence was recently granted to a pub, already known for the noisy violence and vandalism of its clientele in an otherwise beautiful and tranquil place, to stay open to three o'clock in the morning, as if an opportunity to drink in public until such a time was what the local young people most needed. One hopes that the council that granted the licence was corrupt, in the pay of the brewery that owns the pub; for at least if it was corrupt, its decision was motivated by something with which we can all identify, namely the desire for quick and easy self-enrichment. That is human, all-too-human. On the other hand, if it was because the council thought it was a desirable thing in itself – no, I cannot bring myself to entertain such uncharitable thoughts about the stupidity of my fellow-beings.[17]

The editor of *Le Constitutionnel* did not think much of the constitution, at least as then exemplified by elections in Jersey, which he said gave rise to perpetual nuisance, backbiting, calumnies, jealousies, beatings, hatreds of every kind, and general disorder both public and private.

Unfortunately for the *éditeur-Jésuite* of the Journal of Public Good, and fortunately for that of the *Chronique*, the former was accused a little later in the year, still in the midst of the controversy over the Le Gendre murder, of having received stolen goods at his bric-à-brac shop. Needless to say, the *Chronique* lingered lovingly over this story, never using one word where a hundred would do:

> When we represented the Editor-Jesuit of the *Constitutionnel* as the living personification of the type upon whom Eugene Sue based the character of Rodin[18], we did not yet know in Truth just to what extreme depths this ignoble creature was capable of dragging baseness... Rodin pales by comparison...

Rodin, it is true, was false, perverse and wicked; but at least he would have recoiled from publishing his own shame... It seemed then that there still existed in the soul of this filthy Jesuit some shadow of decent sentiment... [But] the editor of The *Constitutionnel* shows a cynicism which is perhaps without precedent when he publicly proclaims a fact that, even according to his truncated account, ought to make him blush – if his soul had not already renounced all sense of delicacy. 'I don't care what is said of me!' he cries. Indeed, when one has descended to the last rung of the contemptible, one is no longer accessible to shame!

But let us pass now on to the facts about which the editor of the *Constitutionnel* has had the audacity to publish a long article in his last edition. It appears that this man, whose venal pen is at the service of all who will employ him for a little money, – even when it is a matter of making secret complaints against the conduct of a Magistrate politically attached to the political party that the *Constitutionnel* represents[19] – practises simultaneously the profession of editor and bric-à-brac dealer, that he modestly calls *brocanteur*; but to which, if he had consulted a rhyming dictionary, he could have give a name both more applicable and true.[20] Now a little while ago some chicks, an iron bar and a pickaxe were stolen from M. Gosset; last week, some of M. Gosset's employees saw the said pick in the window of the dirty hovel situated in the dark street at the top of Hilgrove Lane, inhabited by the editor of the *Constitutionnel*: the cloaca that he dignifies with the name of *boutique de brocanteur*! M. *le Centenier* Chevalier[21] having been informed of the circumstance, felt at first some repugnance at going to this disgusting and filthy place; but in end, his duty as a senior Police Officer was imperative, and he decided to go on Wednesday morning and seize the stolen object. The *éditeur-brocanteur* was not at home – he was passing several days on the nearby coast of France – but one of his children said to the *Centenier* that his *noble* father had bought the pick for 30 *sous* from an Englishman who was unknown to him. This tool, which cost about 6 shillings, was immediately identified by M. Gosset's workers, although the name of the owner, deeply imprinted on the handle, had been carefully removed after the theft. The *éditeur-brocanteur* forgot to mention this circumstance in his article; but it is worth mentioning because the mutilation of the handle to make the name of the owner disappear ought necessarily to have given rise to suspicion about the legitimacy of the possession of the instrument in the hands of an unknown person!... Be that as it may, the *éditeur-brocanteur*, having returned to Jersey in the afternoon of the same day on which the pick was seized, M. *le Centenier* Chevalier paid him a visit the next day, accompanied by another police officer, with the aim of obtaining more information. He asked him how much he had paid for his tool, and to indicate the person who had sold it to him; but our Rodin, who has a memory shorter than his child's, replied that he did not remember the price he had paid, nor did he know the individual from whom he had bought it; but in any case, it was for M. Chevalier to find the thief, since it was his job.

Now, let us ask, is there a single merchant of good faith who would reply in this way? Where is the man with the least self-respect who, finding himself in this annoying and painful position, would not make immediate efforts to help the police find the thief, so that he might be brought to justice? All the honest classes of society have an interest in the arrest of thieves; and in this case the *éditeur-brocanteur* should have shown all the more desire to help the police since it is not the first time stolen objects have been found in his shop... Not later than last year, the deceased Centenier Le Cronier stated in one of his reports presented to the Court that he had seized a shirt that had been stolen at an inn at M. Jean De La Croix's, and then sold for a shilling to the said de la Croix.[22]

The righteous indignation of the *Chronique* then mounts, so that before long the article addresses itself not to its readers, but to the supposed miscreant:

Certainly the reply given to M. Chevalier by the bric-à-brac dealer would have justified that officer in arresting him immediately... However, he did not, in the hope that this individual, through some slight self-interest, would decide to find the thief; it was therefore only on Friday that M. Chevalier, who had consulted the *Procureur-Général*, decided to arrest the *éditeur-brocanteur* [editor junk dealer] on the charge of having bought the stolen pick at a low price – and this only after another refusal to find the man who had sold him this thing... However, this low writer, in announcing his arrest with an incredible audacity, did not fear to attribute it to vengeance! But wretch! If M. Chevalier had wanted to show severity towards you, he would have arrested you on

Wednesday, and not accepted the payment of bail. It was only on Friday, after having given you time for reflection, that he arrested you, and yet still be so indulgent as to accept the bail paid by the owner of the broadsheet that your editing has dishonoured and rendered the opprobrium of journalism.

A footnote – who can imagine such a scholarly device in a newspaper article of today? – generously concerns itself with the fate of the rival newspaper:

The *éditeur-brocanteur* observes in part of his article that if he stops editing *Le Constitutionnel*, this journal will remain the same. This is almost impossible, because no other writer could be found who would attach his name to degraded an editorial policy. There was a time when the *Constitutionnel* was written and edited by sensible men, who knew how to reason and to argue, but for about two years this poor journal has been entrusted to the care of an editor without principles and to a little cabal of men who are bitter at their loss of the public employment that made them comfortable[23], and it has fallen into a state of degradation without equal. It could only benefit from a change of editor; but unfortunately the owner seems to suffer from a kind of apathy that prevents him from seeing that it would have been in his interest to dismiss the *brocanteur* and his cronies, and replace him by a conscientious editor who would demonstrate how to raise this journal in the esteem of the public.

In the opinion of the *Chronique*, the conduct of the editor of the *Constitutionnel* represented a public danger:

What! The police find a stolen object in the possession of an individual that he has bought for a quarter of its value, and when he is asked from whom he bought it replies, 'It's your job to find out!' If this is permitted, thieves will have a good time... To say that the purchase of stolen goods is not a crime, that it entails no criminal responsibility, would be to smooth the path of brigandage, to give *carte blanche* to thieves. We are not yet there, thank God; and we hope that we shall not be for a very long time.[24]

Oddly enough, after this outpouring of vituperation, the matter was dropped from the press. As far as I have been able to discover, neither the *Chronique* nor the *Constitutionnel* referred to it again. De La Croix appears not to have been brought to court, let alone punished; or, if he was, it was not reported. But it is difficult to believe that, in such an event, the *Chronique* would suddenly have become reticent or desirous of sparing the feelings of its *bête noire*. I can only conclude that the outcome of the affair was embarrassing for both sides: for the *Chronique* because its accusations were not provable, and for the *Constitutionnel* because there were enough undispelled suspicious circumstances surrounding the affair that it did not wish to dwell further on the subject. One must call it a draw, then, like the Scottish criminal court verdict of *not proven*.

XVIII

What was not a draw, at least if measured by practical outcome, was the dispute between the two newspapers over the nature of the Jersey police system. Here the wife-beating, stolen-goods-receiving editor of the *Constitutionnel* (if one is to believe the worst of him) scored a decisive victory: the police system of Jersey was soon to be changed forever. Whether for the better is, of course, another question, and one not easily answered.

It was the burden of the *Chronique*'s complaint against its opponent that its constant denigration of the police had led to a loss of respect for them, and therefore to an increase in criminality on the island, of which Madame Le Gendre's murder of Mr Le Cronier was the culmination, the apogee, or the distilled essence.

This is not a completely ridiculous argument, though it is one that is difficult to prove with irrefutable evidence. In contemporary Britain, an enormous increase in the crime rate has been accompanied by a loss of respect for the police: though whether the increased crime rate caused the loss of respect, the loss of respect caused the increase in the crime rate, or there was no connection between the two and it was a mere coincidence, is a matter of dispute.

Jean De La Croix argued persistently for the establishment in Jersey of a professional police force, one that would not only react to crimes when they occurred, but patrol the streets to prevent them from being committed in the first place. The pro-English faction on the island did not want to adopt the English system of policing, instituted fewer than 20 years before by Sir Robert Peel, while the anti-English faction wanted to adopt it. Perhaps this seeming inconsistency is explained by the difference in attitude to the English immigrants and visitors, not all of them of the respectable classes, who were becoming more and more numerous on the island: for the anti-English faction, they were the source of most of the crime, or of the increase in crime. Settled populations have always blamed immigrants for crime, of course, but just because this is a prejudice does not mean that there is never empirical reason behind it, or at any rate in its favour (not the same thing). Of these three killings, only one concerned native Jerseymen alone, a sample too small to be of statistical significance, no doubt, but possibly reflective of the demographic composition both of perpetrators and victims of crime on Jersey at the time. A brief survey of the court reports in the surviving Jersey newspapers suggests that the cases disproportionately involved immigrants and visitors, though this might have been the result of police or reportorial bias.

The editor of the *Constitutionnel* had argued the deficiencies of the police in Jersey long before the murder of George Le Cronier, and therefore was able after the murder in Seward's café to indulge in that most delightful and self-gratifying of statements, I told you so. After the murder of Simon Levi, he wrote[1]:

> There cannot be a cause without effects, and even less effects without a cause. This is an incontestable truth founded on the nature of things themselves. On last Thursday to Friday night, an ambush was committed, a dreadful murder, an atrocious crime, at an inn, or – if you prefer – in a licensed café. The author of this crime left another café where he had gambled and drunk all night in the company of other persons until *two o'clock in the morning*! There you have it, two inns *at least* open at ungodly hours. Who tolerates this state of things? The question answers itself, it is the Police: the Police whose special duty it is to ensure that inns are closed at the proper time, and who ought to have prevented this crime. If the Café Seward had been closed, would the murder in question have taken place? It is more than doubtful.

> It is certain that if Nicolle had not gone at all, he
> would not have returned with vengeance in his
> heart and a gun in his hand.

This passage brings to light a tension in all thinking about crime, a tension that is frequently unresolved even today. On the one hand the person who commits a crime is guilty, for he could have chosen to act otherwise.[2] On the other, there are statistical regularities that seem to imply social forces beyond the control of the mind of the supposedly guilty party. De La Croix's argument is that if you permit people to stay up late carousing, more crimes will be committed as a natural consequence, and therefore blame attaches to those who have it within their power, and even the duty, to forbid such carousing. In this case, it was the culpable failure of the police to close the Café Seward that was a necessary condition of the crime, for (says De La Croix) 'it is more than doubtful' that it would have taken place without it.

De La Croix's argument rests on the correlation between late-night carousing and criminal acts that, to quote Adam Smith, 'is a matter of fact too obvious to require any instances to prove it.'[3] And correlations of this and other sorts have been used to diminish the responsibility of criminals for their acts, by attributing them to social, or sometimes to what might be called socio-pharmacological forces, beyond their control. Poverty is an old favourite, of course; but the will to excuse is antecedent to any empirical evidence that justifies excuse, for when it is shown that poverty is *not* statistically correlated with crime, the alleged cause revealed by statistics becomes not poverty in the absolute, but in the *relative* sense; and when even this is shown to be not the case, then the 'criminogenic' force becomes the increased supply of goods available for theft, in other words *wealth* rather than poverty.[4]

De La Croix argued that the late opening of the Café Seward was the necessary condition of the murder. Does that eliminate or lessen the responsibility for his act of Thomas Nicolle, the man who shot Simon Levi? This is a confusion that often bedevils discussions of crime and the morally appropriate way to deal with it.

Even were it granted that the late-night carousing winked at by the police was a necessary cause of the murder, it was very far from having been a sufficient one. De La Croix himself says that the late opening of the café, though illicit, was regular and repeated, nor (he adds) was the Café Seward the only café in St Helier with late opening indulged or ignored by the police. But murder was, and still is, a very rare event; thousands of late-night carousers in Jersey must have caroused without killing anyone. And the same is true, of course, for all the other social forces that are said to lead criminal acts. The midnight carouser who kills does not kill solely because he carouses, therefore, any more than the unemployed young man burgles simply because he is unemployed; even Thomas Nicolle, the carouser-killer, is likely to have caroused some hundreds of times without a fatal outcome; and if it is held that being in a situation that is known to be statistically associated with a certain kind of criminal behaviour lessens the guilt of the criminal, it might be replied that it actually *increases* his guilt, at least in so far as he put himself voluntarily in that situation in the knowledge of its risks.[5] The evidence suggests that Thomas Nicolle had knowledge by acquaintance of the effects of alcohol on his own state of mind and conduct, and it is extremely unlikely that he knew nothing of its inflammatory properties on the mood of others, since he was said to be an habitué of cafés such as Seward's.

All people act in definite circumstances: there is no possible behaviour that takes place in the complete absence of circumstances, floating free, as it were, of all that has preceded and surrounds it. However, this is not to say that circumstances *determine* behaviour, in the way that the trajectory of a billiard ball struck by another is determined by the laws of mechanics. To quote that great Jerseyman, Karl Marx, 'Men make their own history, but they do not make it just as they please; they do not make it under circumstances chosen by themselves, but under circumstances directly encountered, given and transmitted from the past.'[6] It is a mistake, however, to conclude from this, as many have done, that man is not free, any more than it would be right to conclude from the fact that I inherited English as my mother tongue that my inheritance determines what I say simply because there are words in other languages that do not exist in English. The infinitude of possibilities is not reduced by the closing off of some possibilities; to think so is to mistake the nature of infinity.

This does not mean that Jean de la Croix was wrong in drawing attention to the circumstances in which Thomas Nicolle killed Thomas Hodge. In different circumstances, Thomas Nicolle might have made different choices, without thereby ceasing to be responsible for them. And De La Croix was almost certainly right also in ascribing the worst possible motives for the police laxity and failure to enforce the rules then in force regarding the opening hours of licensed premises. The police did not argue that the freedom to drink in a public place early in the morning outweighed in value the various harms that followed from it, or that the freedom to do something always has its costs. This is an argument against which there can be no conclusive evidence; it is always a matter of judgment as to how much cost is worth how much benefit, a matter over which reasonable people might disagree. In fact, the police argued nothing at all to explain or excuse their inaction; and de la Croix explained it for them *ad hominem*[7]:

> It is the police who frequented the Café, who had taken a meal there together shortly after the election of the *Connétable*... and were it necessary to add how many *louis* the meal cost, we should be able to do so.

Be that as it may, the relationship between late opening hours of licensed premises and acts of violence appears still to hold in St Helier. Seward's Café, in which Levi was shot, became the Hotel de l'Europe, where Marx and Engels used to stay. The boarding house next door in which John Noon stabbed Thomas Hodge to death is now Chambers' Wine Bar, an establishment with a certain local reputation. According to the website of the Merseyside police:

> In the early hours of Saturday, 5th February 2011 the man shown in these images walked up to a male [in Chambers Wine Bar] and, in what seemed like an unprovoked attack, struck the victim across the face with a bottle, causing deep facial injury. The offender is described as having a 'scouse accent'.[8]

XIX

Not only were the police corrupt, according to the editor-Jesuit, but they were cowardly:

> It now remains to consider the manner in which the police conducted themselves in the Café Seward affair. They were made aware of an atrocious crime, and of who committed it.
> What did they do?
>
> First the *Connétable* remained where he was.
>
> Second the *Centenier* Chevalier, accompanied by the *Vingtenier* Fauvel and three of the *Connétable*'s officers, instead of seizing the culprit there and then, left him alone for more than *five hours*! thereby giving him the opportunity to flee − or to kill himself − or to destroy the evidence!! − they limited themselves to stand guard for *five* hours in the street, waiting for the maternal dawn, or rather until the rising sun warmed up their courage!!! Even then, undecided as to who should first enter and penetrate this house to which they had laid siege for *five hours*, it was a *stranger* (!!) who first entered!!!!
>
> Third, not only did the *Centenier* Chevalier have the three persons mentioned with him, but three *night watchmen*, against whom the police had not long before entertained so great a dislike[1]; it was the famous *Lawrence* [one of the night watchmen] who seized Thomas Nicolle, so great was the prudence of the so-proud gentlemen, now become so timid.

Of course, most human behaviour is capable of more than one interpretation, and the *Jersey Herald* lost no time in pointing

out, in refutation of De la Croix's allegations, that the conduct of
the police was not cowardly, but perfectly sensible and prudent;
to have gone charging blindly into a dark house, into a room of a
drunken, enraged man in possession of a gun that he had already
demonstrated that he was prepared to use, would have been the
height of folly, and quite possibly have ended in another, avoidable
death.[2]

Strictly speaking, a single instance of police cowardice (if that
is what it was) would not by itself condemn a whole system, unless
it was believed that there existed a system in which such cowardice
could altogether be avoided. But Man is not only a political but
also a rhetorical being, swayed as much by words as by things:
so that it would have been odd if the supporters of the current
police system had admitted that, yes, in this instance the police
had behaved in cowardly fashion, but had gone on to argue that
in general they did not and in any case there was no reason to
suppose that, if they had been part of a paid force, they would
have been more willing to risk their lives in the performance of
their duty than they had been as unpaid volunteers. After all, there
is at least an etymological connection between *honour*, *honourable*
and *honorary*. Indeed, one could make out a case that, since praise
and gratitude are the only recompense of volunteers, apart from
the satisfaction of doing the work itself, voluntary workers were
more likely to be brave than professional.

The controversy over the role of the press in producing baleful
events such as the murder of George Le Cronier continued for
months afterwards. *Le Constitutionnel* replied to the Accusations on
18 July, 1846:

> The police newspapers, the *Herald*[3] and the *Chronique*,
> both representatives of a retrograde system whose
> aim has always been to blind the people the better
> to mislead them, saw fit last week to use fresh
> invective with which to insult the *Constitutionnel*. The

Herald, above all, sought to persuade readers that the death of *Centenier* Le Cronier was due to the words of some island newspapers, but especially of *Le Constitutionnel*.

Here are the terms in which it wrote:

'The community of Jersey have to thank themselves for all the evil brought upon them by a scurrilous press. It is well known that had two local French journals conducted themselves in a decorous and becoming manner, Mr Le Cronier would not have been murdered by the virago who took her ideas of retributive justice from the "Constitutionnel", and that if an unscrupulous party feeling had not been aroused by an unscrupulous party press, Mrs Le Gendre would never have escaped the penalty due to her crime.'

There are two heads of accusation in this paragraph that are quite distinct: the first is that the woman Le Gendre would not have killed M. Le Cronier without *Le Constitutionnel*; and, second, that without *Le Constitutionnel* the woman Le Gendre would have paid the ultimate price.

In the first place, there is in this paragraph remarkable and cowardly calumny. The envious are always insulters and calumniators: and who could wish for greater ones than the *Herald* and the *Chronique*. There is calumny because no facts could justify these infamous accusations: first because we are ready to prove that, at the time of the inquest on the unfortunate M. Le Cronier, there was no question of blaming the *Constitutionnel*. It was only the next day, the day after the inquest was adjourned, that the *Centenier* Chevalier who, meanwhile, had visited the woman Le Gendre in her cell, on the pretext of removing her irons [in which she was held], came, afterwards, to add to his deposition the following day that this woman told him she had read in the *Constitutionnel* that it was necessary to *take the law into one's own hands*.

Now it is obvious, as we have already proved, and we defy the *Herald* to prove otherwise, it is evident that this woman could not have used those words, second because such a sentence never appeared in the *Constitutionnel*, and third because, if she was wrongly quoted, she would have pointed out the passage where the words she used were to be found.

In coming to add to his precious deposition, on the second day of the inquest as an afterthought, the *Centenier* Chevalier had a purpose that everyone can easily guess: he wanted by this means to denigrate us. Has he succeeded? Not yet!

Was the *Constitutionnel* the only newspaper found at the house of Le Gendre during the police search? No. Several issues of the *Chronique*, the *Herald* and the *Impartial* were found there. The cupboards of *Mulberry Cottage* were full of them. Now during his second deposition, which was more officious than official, *Centenier* Chevalier confined himself to citing only our journal,

By now, of course, rhetorical victory, or at least relief of feelings, was much more important than the discovery of truth[4], and the *Chronique* replied in its next issue, of 22 July, 1846:

That the editor of the *Constitutionnel* continues every week to launch insults against the police of St Helier is not astonishing, since no one can go against his instincts, and his are always to calumniate, to slander. Brought up by charity in a Jesuit seminary, one ought not to be surprised if the education he received – admirably seconded by his naturally low and nasty character – made him one of those disciples of Loyola whose type has been depicted so strongly and truthfully by Eugene Sue! In tracing the character of Rodin in a manner at once so truthful and terrible, one might have said that the author of *The Wandering Jew* must have had the Editor-Jesuit of the *Constitutionnel* before his eyes, whose physical dirtiness, already repellent, is yet surpassed by the baseness and meanness of his moral qualities.

Ad hominem arguments don't come much more *ad hominem* than this. Our modern resorts to insult are, by comparison, genteel and mealy-mouthed, euphemistic and half-hearted, and if we laugh at the Victorians because of their reticence about sex, surely they would laugh at us for our excessive fear of giving offence. The *Chronique* continues, very marginally less *ad hominem*:

To reach his goal, all means for him are good; his lies, calumnies, insults, idiocies stop at nothing... not even the bloody memory of the horrible drama of 27 February last – tragic and deplorable fruit of the baleful tendency of his writings about the police!

If assertion were evidence, all would have been proved beyond reasonable doubt:

If ever there were a subject on which the *Constitutionnel* ought to have condemned itself to an absolute silence, if there is an event that ought to have horrified it, and before which it ought to place a thick veil, it was assuredly the death of the unfortunate *Centenier* Le Cronier, whose generous blood, spilt by an odious monster, has gushed over the journal, read moments before the frightful crime, that decided the murderess to strike her victim!!!

The *Chronique* then decided that a little fairness and magnanimity was in order, and apostrophised the editor of the *Constitutionnel*, only soon to return to its tone of outrage:

Indignation, however, will not render us unjust towards you; we do not accuse you of having foreseen this crime, of having *intentionally* armed the infamous Le Gendre; but it is a fact that you will never be able to deny – a fact that will for ever leave a bloody stain upon your pages – and fact, in short, that has been established beyond doubt – that the reading of the *Constitutionnel* inspired this execrable woman to a redoubled hatred of the police, and that it was under this inspiration that she struck M. Le Cronier! We do not rely for this fact upon the depositions of MM. Chevalier and Manuel, for these two gentlemen are members of the police, whose testimony you would have the impudence to put into doubt; but we do so on a deposition that you would not have the effrontery to accuse of falsity, that of M. *le Docteur* Jones:

'Sunday morning, before the inquest jury had met at the hospital, I went to see the accused in the prison. M. Chevalier and M. Bichard were with me. She said that she felt much better and expressed the wish that I take off the handcuffs that, in my position as surgeon to the prison, I had thought prudent to put on her an hour and a half before, the accused having said that she was mad and having given me to understand that she would destroy herself. She then said, *voluntarily*, that she had taken a knife from the window sill or a table (I don't remember which) and had struck M. Le Cronier saying that if she had to go to prison, it might be as well for something. The following Monday, she repeated the same thing, in the presence also of MM. Chevalier and Manuel, about how she had struck M. Le Cronier, adding that, *as a result of an article she had read in the Constitutionnel, she considered the police had no authority and did not want to do their duty, or words to that effect.*

In the light of this overwhelming proof, of this voluntary statement made by the woman Le Gendre, how does the *Constitutionnel* seek to justify itself? It cites its account of the assault committed by Seward on the person of Le Cras[5], then maintaining that there was nothing in this article that could have induced the Le Gendre woman to commit this crime. But one must bear in mind that this journal was read regularly in that resort of crime and debauchery – that several editions were found there, and that in all of them the police were more or less insulted.

Here the *Chronique* inserted a footnote to the effect that the allegation of the *Constitutionnel*, that copies of the other newspapers had been found in Mulberry Cottage, was 'completely' false. Only one fragment of any of these journals was found there, as those who searched the house had attested in their sworn statements. 'But,' added the *Chronique*, 'one more lie or less is a small matter for the *Constitutionnel*.'

The *Chronique* continues:

But even the article that the *Constitutionnel* quotes with an air of triumph contains a passage that was certainly of a nature to excite the vengeance of the horrible harridan of Mulberry Cottage. Here is the passage:

'If justice appears to be unmotivated, does nothing to suppress such disorders[6], murder will soon be the order of the day, and it will be permissible for the first person who believes himself to have been injured by an article in the press to attack whomever he pleases on the slightest pretext, and to take justice into his own hands. Indeed, when the police are the first to give such an example, one must expect every excess.

The *Chronique* appears not to notice that these lines are not an encomium to violence or to disorder, but a warning against the failure properly to repress violence and disorder, as alleged, almost certainly correctly, in the case of the assault by Seward on Abraham Jones Le Cras. To say if you do not do x, there will be y, is implicitly to state that y is undesirable. It is a warning, not an incitement. This is all perfectly obvious; nevertheless, the *Chronique* continued:

It is easy to conceive the effect that these lines must have produced on the imagination of a woman whose imagination was already inflamed, of dissolute morals, used to crime, and who believed that she had cause to complain of the police because they had resolved to put an end to her shameful traffic! In her state of mind, what more did she need to decide to kill the first police officer who came to her door to do his work?

The *Chronique*'s reflections here become a little more subtle:

> We understand perfectly that articles such as the
> *Constitutionnel* publishes against the police are not
> dangerous to the honest class of society that knows
> how to put them into perspective and understand
> the motives behind them; but unfortunately there
> exists in Jersey, as in every other country, a crowd
> of individuals who live only by theft, by rapine and
> by debauchery. In all countries this class is naturally
> an enemy of the police and of the law, and it is
> inevitable among this class that the *Constitutionnel*
> should exercise its baleful influence; and it is upon
> the minds of this abject and corrupt mass that the
> repeated insults against the agents of authority
> produce a powerful and sometimes terrible effect!
> Indeed, in attacking the police weekly – in painting
> even its most praiseworthy acts in false colours –
> in representing it without let-up as a tyrannical
> body that every day abuses the powers that the law
> confers on it – is it not to excite, to push to *resistance*
> those with whom authority is called upon to deal
> severely? Is it not to work for the overthrow of
> the social order? One must also not be surprised
> if, on reading these articles against the police, the
> murderer applauds, the thief claps his hands, and
> the brawler and the vagabond shouts bravo!

Here in this passage, it seems to me, the *Chronique* has
hit upon a serious and difficult question, one to which no
final answer can be given.[7] If society is to be free and open,
criticism must likewise be free and open; but at the same time,
intemperate criticism can destroy the very conditions of its free

exercise. In other words, criticism can exert a destructive as well as constructive influence; and it can exert a different effect on different parts of society.

If one criticises an institution, what is the correct standard of comparison from which to do so (all judgment being comparative, as Doctor Johnson said)? Usually it is done from an abstract conception of some ideal and perfect institution: a hospital, for example, in which all diagnoses are not only swift but accurate, all the staff are invariably kind and understanding and all treatments are successful; or a police force all of whose members are upright, honest and intelligent, and none of whom have any of the normal human weaknesses that afflict every other member of society. Such institutions never have existed, do not exist and never will exist.

On the other hand, the imperfectability of institutions, as of man, cannot be made an excuse for complete immobilism. To answer every criticism with the reply that nothing and nobody is perfect is to succumb to a lazy fatalism, not least about one's own faults or vices, and an acceptance of evils that could be avoided. To defend from criticism immoderately is as bad, but in a different way, as to criticise immoderately. A correspondent to the *Constitutionnel*, who called himself *Scrutator*, drew attention to the absurdity of defending the police against all criticism, as the opposing journals did, before even M. Le Cronier had been murdered:

> Sir,
> The numerous catastrophes which come to our ears every day and bring desolation to the breast of families are caused by the irregular, insufficient and totally inefficacious system of the police of St Helier, whose population is perhaps of nearly 30,000 souls. In every civilised country, every effort is made to keep pace with the country's progress,

to change every public institution according to the needs of the age; but in Jersey, oh! in Jersey one must not speak of it, on pain of being accused of wanting to lay a sacrilegious hand on what some rather bizarrely call our ancient privileges.

When St Helier had only 4,000 or 5,000 inhabitants, mostly natives of this isle, the system that is so praised today might have been very good; but in 1846, one would have to be of bad faith to maintain that what served in centuries past could harmonise with present times.[8]

Let the taverns be closed at *10 at night*; then let an effective police force be established, that has no political influence; and then we will be able to hope to see Jersey return to the ranks of civilised countries.

One could, of course, pick holes in this. No evidence was presented that Jersey was either more violent than it had been in the past, or was more violent than anywhere else, including those places with paid police forces. A cluster of unusual events, such as three murders in the course of three months in so small a population as Jersey's, is not a sound basis for concluding anything. On the other hand, even if Jersey were no more violent than it had been, and was no more violent than anywhere else, that would not be an excuse for doing nothing, if improvement were possible. And if perfect information were required before action, with an assurance that proposed measures would work precisely as anticipated, no one would ever do anything.

The controversy between the *Constitutionnel* and the other newspapers rumbled on for months. In October, for example, *L'Impartial* ran a headline: 'Advantages of a paid police force – Two murders in a week committed by policemen!'

Le Constitutionnel was quick to reply:

> Even if it were true that there have been two murders
> by *Policemen*[9], which is entirely false, what would
> these two isolated facts prove against the system?
> Could the *Impartial* tell us how many policemen
> there are in England? And without going so far
> as England, would it be necessary to leave Jersey,
> with its admirable system of unpaid police, to have
> heard talk of *three murders* committed in one month:
> and of members of that police who were *afraid* to
> apprehend one of the perpetrators, making use of
> our *private watchmen!!*

Soon afterwards, the *Constitutionnel* declared an end to
hostilities:

> The owner of this Journal believes it is time to put an
> end to the personal disputes on which the *Chronique*
> and the *Impartial* are engaged with us. They can
> interest only those involved; the public can derive no
> advantage from them. That is why he has resolved
> to allow no further articles to appear in the Journal,
> whatever the provocation given by the editors of the
> *Chronique* and the *Impartial*. The contempt of silence
> is worth more than endless recriminations.[10]

This worthy resolution did not last long, however, and old
habits die hard. In the very next issue, that of 31 October, we
read:

> The editor of the *Chronique* has made a notable
> discovery that must cause general astonishment
> among subscribers to his journal, however deep

their credulity, however blind the faith they repose in him...

Next month, on 21 November, the editor returns to form:

If future historians of our little country need information about the events that are happening under our eyes, it is surely not in the columns of the *Chronique* that they ought to seek it; or, if they do, their histories will be as false as the lessons they draw from it.

The editor of the *Chronique* knows [the truth], but it suits him to mislead public opinion, to promote false ideas among the masses, to gratify those who pay his venal pen. In a word, he keeps to his *metier*, and in truth one cannot blame him for it.

Nor, in the event, was there any let up in De La Croix's campaign of vilification of the police. On 26 December, he ran the following story:

One day this week a young woman was seen hanging around a shop. A person entered it with a silk umbrella that she left by the door. When she left the shop, the umbrella wasn't there, and she ran to catch the girl who had taken it. She was brought back to the shop, where the shopkeeper kept her while the owner of the umbrella went to a *Vingtenier*. He was writing in his office, complained that there was something wrong with his eyes, and refused to act. From there, she went to a police officer who, too busy, refused to act; from there to another member of the police, but he was absent. Nobody could be bothered. Admirable police!

One could not entirely blame De La Croix for failing to foresee that the establishment of a paid police force, even a highly-paid police force, would not necessarily overcome the problem of inertia, and that the experience of the lady with a silk umbrella would be repeated in England thousands of times a year more than a century and a half later. For example, when – 160 years later – my wife telephoned because some youths were setting fire to some objects in our front garden, they refused not only to come, but even to record the event as having happened; and when my wife insisted, she subsequently received a phone call from a more senior policemen, telling her that she had wasted the police's time. Did she not know that they had important paperwork to complete? Could they be expected to go round apprehending criminals, when each arrest took many hours to process?[11] Had she no consideration for the problems confronting the police, and the vital tasks that they had to perform? As M. De La Croix would have said, admirable police, that has the time and energy to make such phone calls but not to arrest young arsonists!

XX

Soon after the murder of M. Le Cronier, it was proposed that a monument be set up to commemorate him. Money was collected immediately, but it took two years for the proposal to be carried out.

Even this seemingly innocuous subject was made a matter of controversy between the *Constitutionnel* and the *Chronique*:

> In its remarks on the project of erecting a monument to the memory of M. Le Cronier, *La Chronique*, using its ordinary tactics, that it uses in preference to all others, ascribes to the *Constitutionnel* expressions that it had never used. It claimed that the *Constitutionnel* said:
>
> 'A simple mausoleum would suffice for a police officer; one raises monuments only to heroes, and in perpetuating the name of the victim, a martyr to his duty, one perpetuates that of the murderer.'
>
> We defy *La Chronique* to find in any of our numbers proof that we have ever used such a sentence. This proves a lack of good faith that dishonours any person who has or ought to have a regard for the truth.[1]

The words complained of do not appear in the *Constitutionnel*, and therefore the editor of the *Chronique* made them up of whole cloth, or (perhaps more likely) misattributed them. But there was one very important area of agreement between the otherwise hostile journals, namely than on the character of Madame Le Gendre. Nothing could be said, and nothing was said, in her favour.

She was a monster, a harridan and, above all, shameless. While John Noon was given the benefit of the doubt straight away – 'a man in a moment of madness, of real mental alienation such as results from the deplorable abuse of alcoholic liquor,' etc.[2] – no such benefit was granted to Madame Le Gendre. From first to last, she was a jezebel. Her supposed repentance in the cell in which she was held, where she said that if only she had read Bible instead of the *Constitutionnel* the killing might not have happened, was scheming, not sincere.[3] She fainted several times in court, but both newspapers were agreed that this was a put-up job intended to evade awkward moments in the evidence, delay matters or to arouse the sympathy of onlookers, and were not genuine, physiological faints. It was particularly outrageous that she dressed elegantly for the proceedings. She heard the police report against her without any emotion, yet began to cry when asked to name the lawyer she would like to represent her.[4]

Her conduct remained scandalous even after she had been sentenced to transportation for life. Those who were due for transportation from Jersey to New South Wales, Van Diemen's Land, or Norfolk Island, had first to be taken to England, and this is how the *Constitutionnel* described Madame Le Gendre's departure from her native land:[5]

> Last Thursday, at about 7 in the morning, Thomas Nicolle, William Drury[6] and the only too well-known Marie Le Gendre, condemned to transportation, were taken from prison and brought to the port, to be embarked on the steamer which was going to Southampton, under the guard of the gaoler, M. Kandick. Although the news of their departure was not generally known, a considerable crowd nevertheless gathered *en route*. There was nothing remarkable in Drury's conduct, but the unfortunate Nicolle, his hands chained, looked

sad and dejected; his exterior proclaimed that he
was suffering inwardly, and that his forced exile,
far from his homeland and from those close to
him, was painful; but it was not at all the same
with the woman Le Gendre, whose shamelessness
contrasted so clearly with the others. Her conduct
was so frivolous that one would have said that she
was going on a pleasure trip. Arriving on the bridge
of the boat, she opened a white handkerchief and
waved it to express her adieux to the onlookers
whom she despised, without thinking that a few
hours later she would be deprived of the refined
costume which adorned her person, and relegated
to the dregs of society and forced to submit to a
régime of hard labour.

At the remove of a century and a half, this seems like the gesture
of a spirited, if culpably unrepentant, woman. The scene is an
intensely cinematographic one, many years before the invention of
moving pictures: a woman agitating her handkerchief slightly, in
the Victorian gesture of farewell, from the safe distance of a boat,
at a howling mob (how mobs love to howl!) that would gladly have
torn her limb from limb. How easily, in smiling at this, one forgets
the suffering, the very intense and no doubt dignified suffering,
of Madame Le Cronier, who was destined to remain a widow for
a further 30 years, half her adult life. Naturally, in the course of
so long a period, she would have made her accommodation with
her new condition; she would not recall the murder every waking
moment of her life. But that is very far from the same thing as
forgetting; not only would she have suffered a pervasive sense of
loss – a mental atmosphere or colouring of thoughts – that was
never quite absent from, even if it was not always in the forefront
of, her mind, but surely the memory would have often come upon
her unbidden, suddenly and with a visceral intensity. Madame Le

Gendre's vicious act cut her life in two, a before and an after; and on her very deathbed (if she had a deathbed, not everyone does) the sorrow of the loss, of half a lifetime spent in regret, must have been present in her mind. We may admire Madame Le Gendre's spirit only if we disregard its callousness, and become callous ourselves.

Madame Le Gendre, like all Jersey prisoners destined for deportation, was taken to Millbank Prison in London. There, apparently, she remained spirited, for, said the *Chronique*, she resisted attempts to cut her hair prior to the voyage, such that force had to be used.[7]

Meanwhile, her companion in the transfer to Millbank, Thomas Nicolle, underwent observation in the prison. The result of this was that doctors who examined his mental state 'reported that he is not mad, as a consequence of which the order has been given that he should depart with the first group of convicts for Norfolk Island.'[8]

This suggests a certain scrupulosity on the part of the prison authorities. Nicolle had been reprieved from the death penalty because of the possibility (no higher) of mental alienation. A message must have been sent from Jersey to Millbank to look out for signs of madness. The report in the newspaper gives no clue as to how thorough the examination by doctors was, and since the typology of mental disorder was different then from now, it is possible that by modern standards the examination was cursory and superficial; but, even so, the fact that the matter was considered at all is indicative that, according to the lights of the time, an effort was made to be just towards the condemned man. The severity towards him was not completely unthinking.

The fact that Thomas Nicolle was undergoing medical examination was surprisingly well-known, and the news had spread far and fast. A journalist on Norfolk Island tried to make use of it:

It is painful for us to learn that an unscrupulous journalist of that island [Norfolk Island] had given hope to the honourable but unfortunate father of the condemned man, in causing him to believe that a stupid petition had been drawn up against the legality of the court, the jury and the judgment, having the effect of annulling the procedure and of setting the prisoner at liberty, and even obtained a silver teapot from him [in recognition]. There has, however, been no legal enquiry, only a medical one, thanks to the testimony of several witnesses at the trial, into the possibility that Thomas Nicolle was not in possession of his faculties. But what did that matter to the hack who modestly calls himself the *Expounder of Jersey Law*... He is satisfied if he obtained his silver teapot by raising the false hopes that rendered the blow doubly terrible for the father of the condemned man.

History does not record, however, the extent of the sorrow of Pierre-Marie Le Gendre, husband of the monster, at seeing her go, though Le Couteur's diary states that he cried. What it does record is that after his wife stabbed M. Le Cronier, he 'took flight, and went with all haste to Grouville, perhaps with the intention of embarking on a ship, but, vigorously pursued, he was led back to the town to be lodged in the prison with his disgraceful accomplice.'[9]

While M. Le Gendre had no hand in the murder, he must have been at least at least a willing partner in his wife's brothel business. To adapt slightly the title of a book about the case of Rosemary West, the wife of Fred West, the serial killer of Gloucester who sexually tortured and killed at least nine people and then buried them in and around his small house, he must have known.[10]

172

Having been captured in Grouville and taken back to St Helier where he was lodged with his wife in prison, Pierre Le Gendre appears not to have been charged with anything. He could not, of course, be made to testify against her, and there is no reference to him in the trial, apart from his rather soothing words to his wife when she uttered her threats.

Whatever he felt about his wife's transportation for life, he did not learn much from her near-collision with the death penalty. On 23 May, 1846, *Le Miroir*, another of the newspapers, whose edition for that date just happens to have survived, had the following story, which suggests that the separation did not cause him immense heartache:

> Pierre Marie Le Gendre, who, after the arrest of his wife, and the sale of their goods by court order, has continued, apparently, to frequent several of the former residents [of Mulberry Cottage], had a very lively altercation last Monday evening, with one Bridget Brown[11], who lives with her parents, at the latter's house, on the matter of Le Gendre's watch that he had lost, and that he accused her of having stolen. He even insisted that she was searched in the presence of her father.
>
> The next day the two of them went together to a house near to Mulberry Cottage, where they had been the day before, to check that he had not left it there. The girl returned home on her own and went to bed. That evening towards six o'clock, they came to tell her that Le Gendre was at the neighbouring Cross Keys Inn, and that he wanted to see her. She went there and they had another altercation. Le Gendre removed a scarf from around her neck. They went back to the girl's house, where her sister also was. They sat at different ends of a sofa without

173

talking, when Le Gendre, suddenly going up to her, struck her a blow on the lower back of the head of the unfortunate girl, who let out a horrible cry and whose blood gushed out in large quantities. Her sister saw something larger than an inch across in Le Gendre's closed hand. She states it was a stone and not a knife, because she would have seen the blade.

After having called out to the neighbours, she ran to tell the police. As for Le Gendre, he stayed sitting on the sofa, next to his victim, who was bathed in her blood, for three quarters of an hour, until the arrival of her father. Then he got up and left the house, but the courtyard was full of people and *Vingtenier* Binet arrived just in time.

He made Le Gendre go back in the house, who let himself be handcuffed be led off to prison, without any resistance. He was searched, and a knife was found in his pocket which had no trace of blood on it. As for the girl, M. *le Docteur* Jones having bandaged her, she followed the *Centenier* Du Parc to the hospital.[12]

The *Chronique de Jersey* for 1 August, 1845 reported the case from the Royal Court, and there, it seems, a somewhat different account was given of the affair:

Pierre-Marie Le Gendre appeared under three heads of accusation: First of having assaulted Bridget Brown and inflicted a serious injury on her by knife or other instrument. Second of having inflicted this wound with intent to kill the said Brown. Third with having endangered Brown's life thereby.

Le Gendre was defended by the other great defence advocate of the island, M. Godfray.

M. *l'Avocat* Godfray rose to present the defence, and it goes without saying, he began by criticising the police of St Helier who, he said, wanted to turn an act of no gravity into attempted murder; and for this reason the police report exaggerated in order to blacken Le Gendre, who is regarded by the police as an evil man who dreams only of shedding blood, as much as possible. There was once a time when police reports confined themselves to the facts, but for some time now they had become political, and made into a kind of drama. Once their minds were made up against an accused, it was difficult for them to change their minds, and to judge the imputed facts calmly and dispassionately.

The *Centenier* who submitted the report would have been well-advised to say that it was with a stone that Le Gendre had struck Brown, for a blow with a knife would have inflicted more damage; and it was for this reason [ie to make the matter look more serious] that he said that Le Gendre had used a knife. If this had been the case, however, why did he not search the accused after arresting him? Why was there no search of the room in which the crime was committed? The police put handcuffs on him because he made threatening gestures, and it was only on arrival in gaol that the gaoler searched him. A knife was then found in his pocket, but there was no trace of blood on it, on the contrary, it appeared never to have been used.

175

In her deposition, Mary Ann Brown, who was present at the scene, said that it was with a stone that the accused had struck her sister, and for her part, Bridget Brown did not see a knife in Le Gendre's hand. Mrs Howard, as witness, said that she ran to the room when she heard cries, and saw Le Gendre seated quietly on the same sofa as Bridget Brown, that she was talking to the accused, and that he threatened to do it again if she did not go away. If Le Gendre had wanted to kill the girl, Brown, he would certainly have been able to do so before help arrived; but when Mrs Howard arrived she found him sitting quietly next to her.

It had been proved, moreover, that Le Gendre was drunk, and that it was in this condition that he had threatened the police. But what was extraordinary was that M. Mauger [the *centenier*], on hearing these threats, did not arrest him, but moralised with him instead. Moreover, what reason could le Gendre have had for wanting to kill Bridget Brown? No witness testified that they had quarrelled; the woman Claire had seen the accused pull a scarf from the shoulders of the girl Brown, saying that it belonged to him, but the girl said that it was she herself who took it off. Le Gendre claims that he punched Bridget Brown, and that she fell on to the fender, wounding the back of her head; but he denied having struck her with a knife, or of having the intention to kill her. M. *le Docteur* Jones, who treated the girl Brown, deposed that he had never looked on her injuries as dangerous, at any rate only if a complication set in, which it could.

The court had to acquit Le Gendre, therefore, because it was proved that he had not struck the girl

Brown with a knife. It was true that the accusation
added 'or another instrument,' but even if he had
hit her with a stone, that could not be called an
instrument.

Not surprisingly, perhaps, M. *le Procureur-Général*, the Attorney-
General, did not accept this weak, logic-chopping and *faute de
mieux* argument:

The defender has claimed that the accused ought to
be acquitted because he struck the girl with a stone
instead of a knife. This principle is monstrous.
Once it is accepted that a serious injury has been
inflicted, it does not matter what instrument was
used to inflict it.

Pierre-Marie Le Gendre was found guilty, though whether of
all three charges, or only of one or two of them, the reports in
the newspapers do not say. It is difficult to believe that he really
intended to kill Bridget Brown (if, indeed, he was found guilty of
that charge), for a single blow on the back of the head with a
smallish stone is not a likely way to kill anyone. Nor is sitting on
a sofa for 45 minutes next to the person one has allegedly just
wanted to kill very likely: though it is important to remember that
the intent of injury with intent to kill is of the moment the injury
is inflicted, not afterwards, when one might have thought better
of it. The charge that, whatever his intentions, he undangered
Bridget Brown's life was not very sustainable, either. It is true that
in those days almost any injury could lead to fatal complications,
by infection for example, against which there were no antibiotics
or other effective treatment. Fatal septicaemia could follow a mere
pinprick. But, as it happens, a scalp wound (which is presumably
what Pierre Le Gendre inflicted on Bridget Brown) is of all wounds
the least likely of practically any wound to become infected,

177

because of the scalp's rich blood supply. Dramatic and messy as Bridget Brown's wound must have appeared because of that rich blood supply, it is likewise impossible that she would have died of loss of blood from it, for clotting always supervenes and puts an end to the bleeding, so that the charge that her assailant put her life in danger could not be sustained in a modern court.

Le Gendre was sentenced to two months' hard labour, and five years' banishment from the island. In fact he was French in origin, rather than a Jerseyman; in the 1841 census he is described as having been a farmer by profession, which is not difficult to believe. He certainly did not follow his wife out to Van Diemen's Land because, as it says in *Le Miroir*, 'the punishment to which she was condemned affected him much less than the loss of his furniture.'

Le Gendre seems to have been particularly attached to his furniture, in fact:

> On Tuesday, he went into the shop of a merchant of this town, took out the knife from his pocket, opened it, and said he would stab the first official who came to seize his furniture, and made several threats against members of the police against whom he believed he had reason to complain.

Mr and Mrs Le Gendre surely had something in common, namely an ability to issue blood-curdling threats which they were prepared to carry out. It is perhaps not altogether surprising that two such sulphurous individuals did not love each other dearly, and that Mr Le Gendre preferred the possession of his furniture to the company of his wife.

XXI

The editor of *Le Miroir* was Charles Romeril, son of the editor of the *Chronique*. Despite this – or was it because of it? – his line on the police question was exactly that of Jean René De La Croix, the ferocious ideological opponent of his father. Whereas Francois Amice Romeril supported the police system of Jersey, his son excoriated it. Was this difference a genuine difference of opinion, or merely an attempt by the family to make sure that it covered all corners of the Jersey newspaper market? (Francois Amice Romeril had even started an English language newspaper, the *Jersey Gazette*.) It is impossible at this distance to tell, though generational reversals of ideological opinion are by no means unknown: my own father was a communist, at least in theory, while I was strongly anti-communist. I still believe that reason, justice and evidence were on my side, but I would not be honest if I denied that the thought had occurred to me that, if my father had been strongly-anticommunist, I might have been more sympathetic to communism. Opinion has its reasons which the mind knows not of: to parrot the opinions of one's father, be they ever so reasonable, is often felt as a failure to have become one's own man.

Indeed, one senses in the vehemence of the *Miroir*'s language a family quarrel being settled, rather than a mere disagreement over a matter of some, but not of infinite, importance. Referring to the press which supported the then-current police system ironically as '*la bonne presse*', the *Miroir* wrote in the wake of the crime committed by Pierre-Marie le Gendre[1]:

> In reporting the arrest of Le Gendre, *La Chronique* put *Another stabbing* in capital letters at the top of its article, and ended thus: 'All this is the one of the consequences of the verdict of the Grand Jury in the trial of the woman Le Gendre.'

The *Miroir* then lays into *L'Impartial*, as a metonym for the *Chronique* that is edited by his father:

> *L'Impartial* openly attributes Le Gendre's deed to the verdict of the Grand Jury. It believed itself to be sublime, when it was only being ridiculous. Here are the words in which it passes judgment on it: 'Baleful verdict! Wretched jury! See into what state you have plunged the country! Crime now walks with its head erect and defies authority and the majesty of the law!'

The *Miroir* goes on to mock:

> The public has completed the sentence, in adding to it, *Poor Impartial! Wretched Impartial!* Is it only since the trial of the woman Le Gendre that there have been stabbings, real or imaginary? No... We pointed out even before the verdict that stabbings had played their part in the columns of the *bonne presse*. We shall prove it.

The *Miroir* then provides a chronicle (derived from the newspapers) of relevant events in relation to the verdict passed at the beginning of May, 1846, to prove that it did not have the effect claimed:

> 2 December, 1845: a boy named Queen stabbed another boy.
> 12 December, 1845: Noon stabbed Hodge to death.
> 3 January, 1846: The *Chronique* reported that a musician had stabbed someone else.

9 January, 1846: Nicolle arrested and charged with the murder of Levy (or Levi).

27 February, 1846: Le Gendre stabbed Le Cronier to death.

12 March, 1846: A man threatened the police with a knife who were trying to rescue him from an accident.

14 March, 1846: *Centenier* Chevalier arrested a man called Kerlate who had threatened his wife with a knife.

20 March, 1846: Nicolle sentenced to death.

27 March, 1846: A man called Gilbert was arrested for having threatened his wife with a knife.

2 April, 1846: O'Toole and Crocker were sentenced to two weeks forced labour for having threatened the police.

The *Miroir* then points out that the *bonne presse* did not attribute the murders of Simon Levi or the *Centenier* Le Cronier to the fact that John Noon had been found guilty only of 'voluntary homicide' and sentenced to only seven years' transportation. Another case had no effect:

> Oh no! Not even the assault on March 2 at the bottom of George Street committed by a relative of a friend of the police, who was arrested for having wanted to plunge a knife into the body of the owner of the inn, and kept a prisoner until the following Thursday and was then released at the request of his family. None of these crimes was an effect of the verdict in the Noon case. No; villains did not reason then; but after the Le Gendre verdict, it was completely different, they all became logicians.[2]

This is not, perhaps, quite fair. It was obviously true that resort to the knife and other forms of violence was not unknown in Jersey before the Le Gendre verdict; but a series of lenient verdicts might very well have a different psychological effect from an isolated one, especially if among the lenient verdicts is one towards the killer of an officer charged with upholding the law. Noon, Nicolle and Le Gendre 'escaped' the supreme penalty that might well have been theirs; and the impression thereby given that the authorities had lost their taste for rigour, or at any rate the confidence to act with it.

Whether or not the lenient verdicts (and commutations of sentences) had any long-term effect on the commission of violent crime in Jersey could obviously not be determined in the short interval between Le Gendre's acquittal from the charge of murder and the appearance of the article in *Le Miroir*. One would have to examine the records of, say an entire year before, and an entire year after. But even this would not be sufficient, for random fluctuation in rates of such events as violent crimes are likely to occur, and in any case other causative factors might be important, for it is seldom in social reality than only *one* thing changes. Moreover, it would have to be shown that the verdicts in question were different in severity or leniency from those that preceded them, that it was a *change* in punishment regime that led (or rather, that *might* have led) to a change in the rate of violent crime. And certainly there is evidence that commutation of the death penalty in Jersey was nothing new. In the *Chronique de Jersey* for 15 October, 1836, for example, we find the following about the commutation of the death penalty for murder of Francois Caillot:

> We hope that the commutation was not on the grounds of mental alienation but on those of opposition to the death penalty – for if he was mad, he should have been acquitted.

Caillot killed his lover when he saw her openly caressing another man – though, as is often the case with jealous men, he was not entirely faithful himself, since he was himself married at the time. Initially depicted in the press of the island as a homicidal maniac, his sentence was supposedly commuted to transportation for life because it was felt that the Bailiff had been biased against him and there were irregularities in the trial.[3] If so, the commutation was of peculiar legal logic: we still think you're guilty, but the judge was biased against you and you haven't received a fair trial, so we will give you a lesser sentence as a compromise. Justice here seems like a bargain made in a middle-eastern souk, rather than an objective process: but perhaps it always is.

What is certain is that there were few executions for murder carried out in Jersey in the century between 1807 and 1907. Here is a list[4]:

1807 William Hales, crime unknown.

1829 Philip Jolin, patricide.

1866 Francis Bradley, murder.

1875 Joseph Philippe le Brun, murder of Nancy, his sister. His was the last public execution in the British Isles. His guilt is in doubt.

1907 Thomas Conan, murder of Pierre Le Guen.

Since there were 60 murders known in Jersey during this period[5], it is clear that the death penalty was carried out only infrequently, sporadically and possibly randomly.[6] A sequence of three killers, none of whom was hanged, was therefore not only common (in relation to the number of murders), but the norm.

But even this does not quite settle the matter as far as the *Chronique*'s and *L'Impartial*'s argument is concerned. Murder was committed in Jersey in the 19th century once every 20 months on average[7], and it is clear that leniency towards three murderers exercised over five years would be different in its effect upon the public mind from that exercised over only three months. Man by nature thinks anecdotally rather than statistically[8], and it is therefore not surprising that a cluster of rare events should have so excited and alarmed many Jerseymen of the time, and might very well have given the impression that the death penalty had been abandoned by the authorities. Had I been alive at the time, I suspect that I would have sided with the *Chronique* and the *Impartial* on the matter of leniency, though perhaps the *Constitutionnel* and the *Miroir* had the better of the argument on an intellectual level, but with the *Constitutionnel* and the *Miroir* on the matter of the police. The problem with political choice, of course, is that of the box of chocolates; one has to buy the whole box on offer, even if it contains items for which one does not care.

XXII

Much had been written, no doubt accurately, on the horrors of the transportation system. It is therefore worth looking at the fate of our three transportees from Jersey: though they were transported towards the end of the system, when conditions had probably ameliorated.

Of John Noon's fate, we can only surmise. It is possible that he was already familiar with Tasmania, because we read in columns of the police report in the Hobart *Courier* for 17 May, 1845, that 'John Noon, an articled seaman of the *Joseph Wheeler*, charged with mutinous conduct on the voyage from Liverpool, discharged, there being no Admiralty Court here. Magistrates can only punish disorderly conduct of seamen for acts committed in harbour.'

In this little item there is something very important and easily-missed, namely that the rule of law had been transferred to the distant colony. John Noon had probably broken the rules on board ship, possibly even in a serious fashion, but the magistrates in Hobart were careful not to break the rules themselves by exceeding their jurisdiction. This self-limitation by authority is a great cultural achievement, and one that in my view is fast being reversed.

John Noon, like Pierre-Marie Le Gendre, was not cowed by his near-encounter with the law. In the *Colonial Times* of 20 May, 1845, that is to say three days later, we read:

> John Noon and Joseph Jenkins, seamen on board the *Joseph Wheeler*, a brig from Liverpool, were sent to the tread-mill for fourteen days, for being absent without leave.

This breach, apparently, *did* come within the remit of the magistrates, for the two seamen must have been absent without leave in Hobart, and they, the magistrates, reacted with what seems to us today great harshness or even ferocity (anyone who has actually seen a treadmill will know that two weeks upon it was no light punishment).

But was this John Noon the same John Noon who was sentenced to seven years' transportation? There are reasons, though none of them conclusive, for thinking that it might have been.

I thought that John Noon would be a common name, but in a search of the Tasmanian archives to find out more about the fate of the killer transported from Jersey I found no person named John Noon had died in Tasmania in any of the decades when 'my' John Noon might have died there. Not only did 'my' John Noon not die there (unless he changed his name), but no other John Noon died there either. So perhaps the name was not so common after all.

Moreover, reports of John Noon state that, when he killed Thomas Hodge, he had just returned from a long journey. There was a John Noon in Hobart in May, 1845, and there was a John Noon, who had just made a long journey, in Jersey in December, 1845. It would be more of a coincidence if they were not one and the same John Noon than if they were. And what more natural than that an Irish seaman − John Noon was Irish − should have taken ship in Liverpool, which is where the brig *Joseph Wheeler*, upon which the Hobart John Noon sailed, was registered.

Finally, the Hobart *Courier* for 27 May, 1846, carried an extensive report of John Noon's crime, reprinted from the *Jersey Times*:

> Sitting himself down in the very midst of the company, he forthwith began to use language which ordinary decency would prevent us from repeating; oaths and imprecations, and the most obscene epithets, flowed from his lips in the most admired rapidity.

Considering that Tasmania was a convict colony, this appeal to linguistic gentility might appear almost comic; but presumably the *Courier* was aimed at the non-convict class that was anxious to maximise the distinction between itself and the convict class.

Why should the Hobart *Courier* have carried news of a banal sailors' brawl, of a type that must have occurred pretty often all over the world, in Jersey? Surely the most likely hypothesis is that the name of the killer, John Noon, was familiar to inhabitants of Hobart. It is true that the article does not draw attention to Noon's previous presence in Hobart, but perhaps he was so notorious a roustabout that it was not deemed necessary to do so. Magazines that concern themselves with the lives of celebrities, after all, often refer to the subjects of their articles by means of diminutives, without explaining who they are: the reader is assumed to know.

The name John Noon appears, in connection with crime and disorder, several times in the Australian press. The first occasion was in the *Sydney Gazette* for 7 January, 1840. There he went before the magistrates' 'drunken list', and was sentenced to two hours in the stocks. On that occasion, one Daniel Carroll pleaded guilty, for more than the fourth time, to drunkenness, and was sentenced as 'a rogue and a vagabond.' On 26 January, 1844, according to the *Sydney Morning Herald*, a John Noon was committed for trial on suspicion of stealing (on that date, Catherine Kenny was sent to 'the Factory' for three months for 'streetwalking and suspicion of stealing.' John Noon was found guilty on February 8, and sentenced to two months' imprisonment in Darlinghurst gaol.[1]

On 15 March, 1862, the *Argus* of Melbourne, Victoria, reported that a John Noon was indicted for stealing from a person, but discharged because the prosecutor had sailed for New Zealand. The other business of the courts consisted of, *inter alia*, the following crimes and misdemeanours: robbery in a house of ill-fame; drunkenness while in charge of a horse; impersonating a detective; stealing a cape; fighting in the street; obscene language; robbery in company; being illegally at large; and uttering and forgery. Whether it is the same John Noon I cannot say; in fact, *our* John Noon had been transported to the Turk and Caicos Islands, and then Bermuda, not Australia, for seven years, but would have had time to return there by 1862. The same newspaper reported on 31 July, 1869 that a John Noon 'was charged with attempting to stab Alfred Tong':

> The prosecutor stated that he was passing along Queen-street at two o'clock on Thursday afternoon when he met the prisoner disputing with a woman. He interfered on behalf of the woman, when the prisoner drew a knife and made a thrust at him. The Bench fined the prisoner 10s for being drunk and disorderly.

This seems very lenient in the circumstances, all the more so if the John Noon is *our* John Noon who has already stabbed someone to death. And if it *is* the same John Noon he was clearly one of those intractable people who learns slowly, if at all, from hard experience: rather like young James Vautier who was sent to the General Hospital in Jersey aged 19 in 1833, his record stating:

> This prisoner, although young, is a very old offender, having been whipped 5 different times in the public gaol and undergone several periods of imprisonment. He was, with several of his companions, sent to the General Hospital for want of sufficient proof to warrant his committal.

Four days later we read:

> Made his escape from the hospital, where he had been sent on the 10th ultimo., has recommenced his usual depredations.

Later in the year we learn:

> James Vautier, Theft, 07-12-1833. To be privately
> whipped.

In 1836:

> James Vautier: two months' hard labour, banished
> for life.
> Escaped from prison by breaking through the wall,
> 23-03-36.
> Returned of his own accord 26 March.
> Escaped 2nd time 02-04-36 and returned 04-04-36.
> Escaped 31st July and returned 4th or 7th August.
> Put Vautier in irons for having impaired his Cell.
> Sent on the Saumarez for the Hulk 13-11-36.

No more is heard of him. Was John Noon of the same type?

XXIII

What of Thomas Nicolle? The change in his manner during his imprisonment, to that of a quiet, well-behaved, pious person, overcome by guilt in the presence of his wife, suggests that his mental problems, in so far as he had had any, were most likely caused by drink. Once separated from it, his behaviour changed, at least after a short time. Does that mean that he was the victim of a disease called alcoholism, that is to say a disease like any other? I do not think so.

Certainly it is within the experience of every practising doctor – to say nothing of that of the general population – that drinkers appear to be different people when they are in drink. A man who is a lamb when sober may be a ferret when drunk. Moreover, he is said to 'lose control' over his drinking: the drink takes him, rather than the other way round.[1] But is it a loss of control, or an absence of will to control – because the drinker likes the life of drinking and prefers it to any other, or at any rate fails to stop to think about it? Again, it is within the province of experience that many addicts abandon their addiction under the influence of a profound shock: a loss, a death, an imprisonment, a tragedy of one kind or another. And if they can choose then to change their behaviour by taking thought, they could have chosen to do so earlier by having taken thought. That they did not take thought is a sign of levity, not of incapacity. Of course, other addicts use such a shock or tragedy to do precisely the opposite, to consume more of whatever it is that they are addicted to. But an increase in consumption is as much an effort of will as a reduction.

In which direction did Thomas Nicolle turn? The fact that he sobered up in prison hardly counts as evidence, for presumably he had little choice in the matter. There is evidence that he did not calm down completely or at once, and rebelled mildly against his fate. Departing London on 25 October, 1846, he arrived in

190

Tasmania (not Norfolk Island, to which the Jersey newspapers had said he was bound) on 17 February, 1847, that is to say a year after his offence. *En route*, he was said to have been insubordinate and was sentenced to 18 months' hard labour, no light punishment; he was also sentenced to 10 days' solitary confinement for 'misconduct.'[2] But I like to think nevertheless that his murder of Simon Levi changed him once and for all; not because Simon Levi would then not have died in vain (for the value of one man's life cannot be set or measured at the price of another man's abandonment of drink), but because it would indicate that redemption, of which we all stand in need, is possible. The redemption does not cancel out the crime, much less justify it, but rather reassures us that we are fully human, that is to say that our conscious thought, moral reflection and will count for something.[3]

In fact, I have been able to discover little of Thomas Nicolle's subsequent career. His son, Thomas Payne Nicolle, born in August 1846, that is to say not long before Nicolle was transported, and later wrote in a letter that he had dropped the name of Nicolle and now went by the name of Thomas Payne, because of his father's crime; he also had decided not to marry because of it, presumably under the impression that criminality was hereditary and it would therefore be best if the line died out.

Thomas Nicolle was pardoned on 16 September, 1856. In 1859, still in Tasmania, and having been pardoned and become a free man, he married a woman called Charlotte Shaw. They had a son, Thomas Shaw Nicolle, born in 1859, presumably conceived out of wedlock and a daughter, Catherine, born in 1861. (Nicolle's first wife remarried likewise, but only in 1867.) Nicolle died in 1864, having moved to New Zealand. Was his second marriage bigamous, did he divorce or did the laws of Tasmania wink at such irregularities? Of his life otherwise – how he made his living, who his friends were, how he died – I have discovered nothing. This failure was for me melancholy, for it brought home to me in a visceral way what, of course, I have long understood intellectually, namely the evanescence of human life, the fleetingness of its joys and pains and struggles. Surely Thomas Nicolle's life as a freed man in Tasmania (or, in fact, wherever in Australia he went) could not have been an easy one, must indeed have been one full of passion and emotion, failure and perhaps success. But it left no trace on earth, at least no traceable trace, unless the existence of descendents be such. And then I think of my own life, with its crises, sufferings, passions and miniscule triumphs, that seemed to me at the time so significant and so important, all gone, soon to be forgotten as if they had been of no account whatever, all ploughed by time into its fathomless waters, and 'deep in the bosom of the ocean buried.'

XXIV

Then, finally, there was Madame Le Gendre. Rather more is discoverable about her, though still so little that it does not amount to even a thin description of her life; the facts are more like the fractions of bones that palaeontologists or anthropologists discover, and from which they attempt to reconstruct the whole animal or man.

She arrived in Tasmania on 4 January, 1847, on the female convict ship, the *Elizabeth and Henry*, after a journey lasting 109 days.[1] Convicts were separated and shipped by sex, no doubt for both moral and practical reasons.[2] Her religion was Church of England. Her disciplinary record contains a bureaucratic description of her appearance: Height, 5' 2¼"; Complexion, swarthy, freckled; Head, oval; Hair, dark; Whiskers, nil; Visage, oval; Forehead, low; Eyebrow, dark; Eyes, grey; Nose, high, long; Mouth, medium; Chin, ditto.

One may wonder what a medium mouth and chin are like; presumably what is meant is 'nothing remarkable.' There is in this description the beginning of the Berthillon system, the anthropometric system of Auguste Berthillon, the French detective, that he invented in the 1890s just before the use of fingerprints for identification was discovered, according to which a few measurements or features of a person's body were sufficient to distinguish him from every other person on earth.[3]

And in the description of her brow as low, we have a faint foretaste of the criminal anthropology of Cesare Lombroso of 40 years later, according to which criminals had physical stigmata of degeneration. These were (*inter alia*) a heavy jaw, receding brow and long arms.[4] Whatever we may think of criminal anthropology as a science, we still use the term 'lowbrow' in a denigratory fashion, one that implies a connection between a physical feature of the skull and intelligence.

193

Interestingly, there is again no mention of Madame Le Gendre's four front teeth knocked out in a previous incident. Perhaps she had replaced them by prosthesis, or missing teeth at her age were so common as not to be remarkable or remarked upon.

The surgeon reported that she was 'generally well behaved', which presumably meant that she had given up her antagonistic stance towards authority, having learnt the hard way that it was more powerful than she. But she seems to have broken the rules in August, 1847, and again in October, 1854. The record does not say in what way for the latter, and the description of the former is illegible; but they could hardly have been serious, for she was recommended for pardon on 23 October, 1855, and it was approved on 16 September, 1856, the same date as Thomas Nicolle's pardon, that is to say a little more than 10 years after her crime.

She was described as married, but the word was placed in quotation marks, suggesting that she was, in fact, married only in the common law sense, not the legal one. Her husband's name was written as Le Jandre. Her 'real' name was Marie Le Noble, she was able to read and write, and her occupation was described as that of housemaid, plain cook and, in some documents, midwife (presumably, though perhaps not certainly, at the Sairey Gamp rather than the Florence Nightingale end of the market).[5] No *haute cuisine*, then, at Mulberry Cottage, though possibly some experience of terminations of pregnancy.

Madame Le Gendre married a man called William Norman (a free labourer) a year after her arrival in the colony, in 1848. She was described – presumably because she described herself – as a spinster, that is to say one who had never been married; in marrying Norman, she became the stepmother of Norman's son, James, and two daughters. The following announcement appears in the Hobart *Colonial Times* of August 25, 1848, under the heading *Convict Department*:

In accordance with the Act of Council 6th Victoria No.18, I hereby give notice, for the first time, that His Excellency the Lieutenant Governor has been pleased to approve of the solemnization of Matrimony between between the undermentioned parties:- William Norman, free, Mary Ann Le Noble, in private service, both residing in Hobart Town.

J. S. Hampton, Comptroller-General

Her marriage certificate gives his age as 47 and hers as 31, implying that she was born in 1817. Elsewhere her date of birth was given as 1808 or 1811 (as the parish baptism records for Grouville show; perhaps she was trying to appear younger in her new husband's eyes than she was. There seems to have been a certain official laxity about such matters, refreshing by comparison with our age of demanding bureaucratic exactitude.

The marriage of Le Gendre to Norman is interesting for a number of reasons. It was celebrated, if that is not too strong a word for it, shortly into her sentence. This suggests that, at least by then, the transportation system was flexible and might even be described as, in part at least, humane. Of course, prisoners today are still legally free to marry whom they choose while they are in prison[6]; but such marriages cannot amount to much (apart from the psychological support they lend, which should not be underestimated) until the prisoners leave prison. By contrast, Mary Ann Norman, formerly Le Gendre, was able to marry in the fullest sense.

Was her marriage bigamous? That depends, of course, on whether she had been legally married to Pierre Le Gendre. Mrs Baghiani, of the *Société Jersiaise*, kindly went through the 12 parish records of Jersey, searching for a marriage act of this couple, and failed to find one, though L. D. Hurel, in *La lyre exile*, mentions that they were married in 1829, without saying more. They could have married in France, though, for Pierre Le Gendre was French. They later went to the trouble of obtaining a *séparation quant aux biens* (on the very day in 1834 when Madame Le Gendre bought a property in St Peter's), that is to say a legal order that meant that they each kept ownership of the goods that they brought to the marriage, in the event of a divorce not therefore having to share them with the other. I find it difficult to believe that a Victorian court would have made such an order for any other than a married couple, or at least a couple that it believed to be married.

Although one Tasmanian document puts the word married in inverted commas, suggesting some doubt as to the legal status of her relationship to Le Gendre, other documents state baldly that Mary Ann Le Noble was married, with no qualification at all. If the authorities thought or knew that she was married, why, then, was she allowed to claim that she was a spinster? It strikes me as likely that, when there was a distance of several thousand miles between husband and wife, the authorities were flexible about legal niceties. The Victorians may have been less rigid than we like to suppose (we always need someone to whom we feel superior in enlightenment).

There is not much else. William Norman died in Tasmania in 1871. It is possible that Madame Le Gendre remarried: a Maria Norman, described as a labourer's widow, married John Morton Matthews, a coppersmith, in the district of Fingal, Tasmania, on 21 April, 1873. Mathews was 50 years old, Maria Norman was put down as 46. If this was Madame Le Gendre, she now underestimated her age by even more, by 16 years. Since people in Victorian times aged very early by our standards, perhaps a 62-year-old woman could easily be taken to be 46; or perhaps Madame Le Gendre was simply very well-preserved.

A Maria Mathews was admitted as a pauper to the New Norfolk Asylum, Tasmania, on 6 April 1875, dying there six weeks later of 24 May 1875 of heart disease, supposedly at the age of 48, but really (if she was Marie Le Noble and Marie Le

Gendre) aged 64. And there we must be content to leave it[7], except to note that, by strange coincidence, one of her second husband's distant descendants married one of Thomas Nicolle's distant descendants.[8]

After all, many lives of her time left even fewer traces than Madame Le Gendre's.

XXV

Notwithstanding fierce opposition to change, the commission into the criminal law and police in Jersey found in favour of the arguments of Jean De La Croix (of the *Constitutionnel*) and Abraham Jones Le Cras (of the *Hersey and Guernsey News*):

> It appears to us that scarcely any part of the criminal proceedings which we have described is such as to suit the present condition of the inhabitants of Jersey.

The police system, in the commission's opinion, was even worse:

> The police is made up of persons whose principal business is not the discharge of the duty imposed by their character of police officers, and who do not act under the constant superintendence essential to a well-organised system.

It criticised the position of the *Connétable*, who was 'legislator, head of police, prosecutor and magistrate.' Furthermore, he was involved in party conflicts in a partisan way.

In 1853, a paid police force came into being. It was at first modest in size, consisting of 10 men each paid 18 shillings a week, who were elected in parish meetings but who were thereafter not allowed to take part in parish affairs. They were to patrol rather than merely to react when a crime had been committed, as hitherto the police had done; but the system of voluntary police has remained parallel to this day.

Were the recommendations of the commission justified? What, for example, was the effect of the new paid police on the commission of crime in Jersey? In the absence of crime figures, it is impossible to say. In the 19 years before the paid police were instituted, there were 15 murders in Jersey; in the 24 years afterwards, there were 12. I have performed a statistical test to these figures, the chi-squared test, and the difference between the two periods is not significant, that is to say the difference between before and after could easily have arisen by chance rather than as a result of the new policing system.[1] However, it is important also to realise that although the reduction in the number of murders per year (from 0.78 to 0.5, that is to say by more than a third) *might* have arisen by chance, having nothing to do with the institution of the new police force, this does not mean that it *did* arise by chance. A longer period of enquiry, both before and after, might give us a more definite answer; but the longer the period, the more likely also that factors other than the new police force had their effect. As with so many questions, this one is not susceptible to a definite answer; our instinct, mildly affected by evidence, has to answer for us.

Were the paid police less corrupt than the voluntary police allegedly were (and who continued to work alongside them)? Here again it is not easy to say. Even in 1853, 18 shillings a week was not sufficient to put a man out of the way of temptation; indeed, the history of the world would suggest that there is no sum of money large enough to put men out of the way of temptation. Like most human phenomena, the lust for gain is more complex than any simple theory can account for; the honesty or dishonesty of a society is not explicable only by reference to induction. And, as we have seen, the paid police in Jersey sometimes were not above augmenting their pay with a little light procuring. I cannot conceive of George Le Cronier as having been corrupt.

As to the question of the fairness of the trial procedure, of which the commission was very critical, I am far from certain that there was much to criticise. No doubt some of the evidence-gathering did not meet present-day standards; one can hardly imagine a murder weapon being accepted as such in any court today that had been found by a passerby and handed to another stranger who then handed it on to the police, with only a notch carved on to its handle as a means of identifying it later. The opportunities for tampering with material evidence gathered in this fashion were manifold; and there were, of course, no finger-print tests performed on the knife with which Madame Le Gendre stabbed George Le Cronier, let alone DNA tests. But the facts of all three cases in Jersey between December 1845 and February 1846 were scarcely in doubt; and though nowadays the motions of forensic tests would have been gone through as a matter of routine, all they would have done is increase the public expense of the process without affecting its conclusions. In other words, they would have contributed more to aggregate economic demand than to a just outcome. It is rarely, in any case, that the results of such forensic tests are unambiguous and incapable of more than one interpretation: a recent, fairly prominent case, that of Dominique Strauss-Kahn, demonstrates the point. The semen of the former head of the International Monetary Fund was found on the clothes of the woman who accused him, but such a finding established only that he had indulged in some kind of sexual activity. The fact that she had some slight injuries also failed to establish beyond reasonable doubt what had gone on between the two parties, for consensual sexual activity is not (need I tell anyone?) all of the same type. Slight injuries in consensual sexual activity are by no means uncommon; young men in England not infrequently expose to the public view, and with pride, the bruises caused by the bites of their lovers.

Certainly the transcript of the trials gave no impression of being *pro forma*, or held merely to confirm a pre-arranged verdict as demanded by the public or by the authorities. Of course, no transcript can precisely capture the non-verbal communication of witnesses, jurymen and judges, which is why justice requires that witnesses must be seen as well as heard. The tone in which something is said sometimes cancels out or reverses the apparent meaning of the words uttered. Perhaps, then, there was more bias in the trials than appears in the transcripts of them. But two of the three verdicts were unexpected, and more lenient than might have been anticipated. The defence lawyer, Hammond, was not only given every opportunity to develop his arguments in defence of his clients, but was clearly a man of the highest calibre and probity. Though the defendants certainly committed the acts of which they were accused, the prosecution did not have it all its own way; the trial was therefore precisely that, a trial. There is nothing to suggest that the court was in search of anything other than a just verdict.

In one important respect, the trials were vastly superior to any for such crimes that take place today: namely in their swiftness. Most supposed murderers nowadays are not tried for at least a year after the crime was committed; and while the elapse of this period allows for the gathering and sifting of much more material, it also allows for the decay of memory and the elaboration of untruth. To hold a man on a charge of murder for more than 12 months is cruelly nerve-wracking both to the man himself (who may still, after all, be innocent), and to the relatives of his supposed victim. And, in my experience, the last nine months of the 12 of waiting rarely add anything significant to the evidence gathered in the first three. If reasonable dispatch is one of the preconditions for a criminal justice system to be considered not only effective but *just*, then the Victorian system was greatly superior to our own in this respect.

At the time Noon, Nicolle and Le Gendre were tried, defendants were not permitted to appear in the witness box in their own defence. I think in these cases, however, such a prohibition hardly acted against their interests, rather the reverse if anything. It is difficult to imagine Madame Le Gendre making much of a favourable impression in the box. From the reports that we have of her, she might have enjoyed the limelight for the time, batted her eyelids at the jury, the judges and the public gallery, fainted once or twice, sobbed with patent insincerity, and generally shown off; but this performance – for such it would have been – could hardly have done her case much good. If she had been allowed to go into the witness box, as surely she would have insisted upon doing, she would also have gone a little later to the gallows, her mixture of levity, callousness and self-satisfaction having turned the jury decisively against her.[3]

Two of the three killers would have been dealt with more severely – at least in the sense of being found guilty of the greater crime, murder, rather than of the lesser crime, manslaughter – than they were dealt with by the Victorian courts. This does not mean that they would have been punished more severely today; indeed, it is not easy to measure the relative severity of punishment according to a single scale, for we no longer have anything like transportation. Besides, the severity of punishment is highly dependent upon the life experience of the person punished. To be forbidden what one never had and will never have is no great hardship; to be deprived of what one has hitherto taken for granted is a much greater one. There is nothing in the record to indicate whether or not our three killers viewed transportation as great hardship, or whether, on the contrary, it offered them hope of a new and better life.

None of the killers had much by way of extenuating circumstance. Noon probably did not intend to kill, but the law does not require intent to kill for a man to be guilty of murder, only intent seriously to injure, and you cannot while fully conscious stick a knife into a man (several times) without such an intent. Nicolle had no excuse at all, and neither did Madame Le Gendre. Yet Noon was free in seven years, the other two in 10.

All three would have been found guilty of murder today, and all three would probably have served a dozen years in prison. Moreover, when they emerged from a present-day prison they would not have been able to have built up new lives for themselves, as Nicolle and Le Gendre almost certainly did before they were pardoned.[4] This, perhaps, will comfort to those who argue that severity of punishment has little to do with the rate of crime: for the comparative mildness of the punishment meted out to the Jersey murderers[5] was followed by a long period of diminishing crime rates until, scarcely more than 50 years after they were sentenced, Britain, including the Channel Islands, had become as well-ordered, peaceable and crime-free a country as perhaps it is possible for an urbanised country of many millions to be.

But this conclusion is a little hasty. First, our three cases are not necessarily a representative sample, indeed they are unlikely to be. Second, the psychology of murder is different from that of other crimes. Third, no one would argue that the severity of punishment is the only determinant of the rate of crime. If you hold the severity of punishment constant, then an increase in the likelihood of being caught would increase the deterrent effect of the punishment. And there are all kinds of contributory reasons why the crime rate should have declined precipitously in the second half of the 19th century, including the internalisation of respectability as a goal. Punishment nevertheless remains important; you would have to be a criminologist to believe otherwise. In 1900 there were 6.5 prisoners in England and Wales per indictable crime; in 2000 114.[6] It is difficult to believe that this had nothing to do with the 4,000 per cent increase in the rate of indictable crimes committed per head of population in 2000 by comparison with 1900 – an increase that would be even greater if an adjustment for the age structure of the population were made.

XXVI

It is with regret that I now leave my cast of characters, including those with walk-on parts in the drama: the murderers, the murdered, the policemen, the advocates, the journalists, the doctors, the lookers-on, the Home Secretary, Queen Victoria herself.

Having rather casually entered into the investigation, attracted to it by a mere phrase on a tomb in an old cemetery, *une main coupable*, a guilty hand, the hand that struck down George Le Cronier, I found myself in increasing admiration of the society that I was investigating. Not that it was perfect, very far from it; it is hardly to be expected that the historical reconstruction of three murders should reveal people always at their best. And I had to control an incipient sneaking affection for Madame Le Gendre, whose spirited conduct – at a distance of a century and a half – could so easily bring a smile to one's face. Whenever tempted to admire her, I thought back to George Le Cronier's will, signed as his life ebbed away from him, to his absence of complaint or recrimination, to his quiet acceptance of his fate, and to the decades of silent heartache of his widow and possibly of his children: and my affection for her departed. I could respect Madame Le Gendre as she made a decent and respectable new life for herself, at least for a time, in Tasmania (if that is what she did), but I could not warm to her.[1]

By contrast, I warmed to Advocates Hammond and Godfray, who seemed to me to incarnate what lawyers should be and, with the exponential increase in their numbers, so rarely are. I should have entrusted my legal affairs to them without the slightest hesitation, or with the slightest fear that they would act in their own rather than in my interests. As far as I can see, they were upright and devoted to their duty. A society in which such men were prominent could not have been wholly bad or corrupt.

It seemed to me that the trials of the culprits were remarkably fair. Though the facts in each case were well-known and hardly in dispute, I had no feeling in reading the transcripts of the trials that they were in any way merely *pro forma* or the verdicts a foregone conclusion. The defence advocates always had a fair crack of the whip and had no hesitation in using it. From the modern point of view, no doubt, there were deficiencies in the procedure. But I am not convinced that the defendants suffered much by them.

As for the gathering of the evidence, it left much to be desired from the modern standpoint. Imagine a policeman standing in court and saying, 'I got the murder weapon from person *a* who got it from person *b*, and I know the one presented in court is the same one as the one I received because I put a notch in it.' The only attempt at anything resembling forensic science was the matching of the bullets in Simon Levi with the gun in Thomas Nicolle's room (they were compatible); but we should not feel too much contempt for the absence of such evidence, because it is so often equivocal and disputed, even if not really disputable. Cases of fraud and dishonesty by forensic laboratories are by no means unknown, experts often overstate, even grossly overstate, the degree of certainty of their own opinions, and much modern forensic evidence is highly circumstantial and equivocal in meaning, and rarely speaks for itself. Like most of what happened in the past it is open to more than one interpretation – which does not mean that what actually happened *didn't* happen, that there is no truth in itself. The increased sophistication of forensic science does not seem to have resulted in superior rates of detection. In the three cases at least, there is absolutely no reason to think that better evidence-gathering, and more forensic tests, would have made any difference to the fairness of the trials, let alone to their outcome. And anyone who has attended a contemporary British trial[2] could not but wonder whether the purpose of much of the procedure with regard to evidence is more to employ a large number of people and increase expenditure than to increase the fairness of trials.

Although I must preface my forthcoming remarks with an acknowledgement that the three cases I have researched might not be a representative sample, they nevertheless brought into question my assumption that the early Victorians – Queen Victoria had been on the throne only eight years when these trials took place – were unthinkingly harsh, severe or sadistic in their treatment of criminals. Clearly, they did not like applying the death penalty. Much has been written about the horrors of the transportation system to Tasmania, Norfolk Island and New South Wales, and it was coming towards its end by the time these three killers were transported; but in these three cases, it is likely that the system was by no means cruel. Of the three killers, two at least succeeded in making a new life for themselves; it is possible that one continued on his criminal path, but we cannot know this for sure. Certainly, we do not have much right to look down upon the Victorians, our own system combining the disadvantages of expense and ineffectiveness.

In one respect the Victorian Jerseymen were much superior to certain modern Britons. Much as many, probably most, Jerseymen disagreed with the verdict passed on Madame Le Gendre, thought it absurd, wicked and socially destructive, I was unable to discover a single one of them who suggested that there should be another trial in order that she might be found guilty of murder and properly hanged. It seems, then, that they were deeply and viscerally attached to the immemorial idea that a person should be tried only once for his or her alleged crime, that he or she should not face double jeopardy, even when the first verdict is absurd or reprehensible: in other words, they had an excellent prejudice in favour of the principle. Unfortunately in modern Britain, that prejudice seems to have been overturned, at least in certain circles. The intellectually dishonest MacPherson report (by a foolish judge, an unctuous archbishop and an intellectual) into the murder of Stephen Lawrence suggested that the principle be abandoned in certain approved cases – a breach of an immemorial principle that would almost certainly prove the thin end of a wedge, because the principle is so administratively inconvenient. Our system having become corrupt and inefficient, all the writers of the report were able to suggest was the abandonment of the rule of law.[3] One has only to compare, indeed, the MacPherson report with that into the criminal law of Jersey a century and a half before to appreciate the loss of moral and intellectual probity that has occurred, a loss that has almost certainly accelerated or gathered pace in the last two or three decades.

As I investigated the three killings, I came to feel a deep affection and respect for the journalists whose newspapers were so full of the passion and venom that made them a delight to me to read more than a century and a half later. If they had been more staid, and kept to the rules of polite discourse, my time in the library would have been much less entertaining than it was, in fact it would have been no fun at all. They were rude and they were uninhibited, but they were genuinely free men, strong of character: much freer and stronger of character than most of us today. Their character leaps from the page. Although they accused each other of every possible corruption, and of the worst motives, it is impossible to read what they wrote without believing in their sincerity. Admirable society that threw up an Abraham Jones Le Cras, a Jean René De La Croix, a Reverend Perrot and a Francois Amice Romeril at the same time, and sustained (though it was very small indeed, not larger than a minor provincial town) all their newspapers! Compared with the typical modern British regional newspaper, with its tabloid format and articles written for people with attention-spans formed by television, their publications were detailed, informative and well-written. Even if the argumentation sometimes lacked scruple, it was vigorous and accustomed readers to controversy. And is there anyone who does not enjoy a good (or bad) *ad hominem* argument?

Did the journalists serve their readership, and what they called their country[4], well? I think that they did, at least in a certain sense: they were both entertaining and informative. If I had been alive at the time and living in Jersey, I should have awaited the next issue of their newspapers with impatience and excitement. Like the editors of these newspapers, I should not have appreciated the historical significance of the brief paragraphs that were inserted from time to time in their pages about the malady affecting potatoes in Ireland (and Scotland), that seemed much less important than the three murders, but that was to be responsible for perhaps 300,000 times as many deaths. But knowing that the famine that killed so many was then in progress, is it wrong to be moved by the following item that appeared in the *Chronique de Jersey* for 12 August, 1846?

> On Monday morning a bottle was found containing
> a piece of paper on which was written the following
> note:
> 'Sun. Aug the 9th
> From the Mary-Ann of Liverpool.
> We are thus foundered on a rock, and parting with
> the ship. No help near. God bless you. Give my kind
> love to all at home. Never expect to see any of you
> again.
> Yours
> H. Schofield

Murder has continued to engross mankind despite the prevalence of much larger and historically more significant events, and I regret the demise of the tradition of publishing the whole transcripts of trials for a general readership, a tradition that existed in Britain for more than two and a half centuries.[5] It was only natural that the journalists should have taken the three murders in quick succession as some kind of social portent or symptom, as being indicative of something beyond their individual occurrence. Indeed, as we have seen, Abraham Jones Le Cras used them as evidence in favour of one of his many petitions to the London government.

We do the same, seeing significance in exceptional or untoward events: indeed, *I* have done the same. When James Bulger was killed, for example, I took the crime as a metonym for something that was happening, or had happened, in British society, and wrote accordingly. I did this partly because I believed it to be true, and partly because of the exigencies of journalism itself. Murder by children, unlike other crimes in Britain, remained rare; but the upbringing of the perpetrating children, which (without being a complete determinist) one felt must have at least *some* connection with their terrible deed, did indeed cast a light upon British society. The three Jersey journalists were not to know that British society was on the verge of a steep and unprecedented decline in crime, and could not be blamed for not knowing it; three murders in as many months in a population the size of Jersey's must have made it appear quite otherwise.

Was the voluntary and elective police system of Jersey good or bad, in desperate need of fundamental reform or of preservation? Were the voluntary police corrupt and inefficient?

From that point of view, the reformers won hands down. Before long, a paid and professional, if still elected, police was set up. Did it make Jersey a safer and less crime-ridden place? It would be difficult to establish beyond doubt. Though it did not appear so at the time, the whole of Britain was entering a phase of what one might call moralisation. The crime rate fell dramatically in the next 50 years, so that by the time Edward VII came to the throne, the country, though very unequal, had unprecedentedly low crime rates. Public drunkenness fell likewise.[n] It is difficult to believe that this was just because of the increased efficiency of policing, or only because everyone feared to be hauled up in front of magistrates or courts if they misbehaved (though they *did* fear it, as much for fear of loss of reputation and respectability as of the resultant punishment). We have surely learnt, never better than in Britain of the last 20 or 30 years, that the increased professionalisation of public employment does not necessarily lead by itself to increased efficiency.

At first sight, the policing of Jersey in the first half of the 19th century appears not only amateur but amateurish, hardly suited to a rapidly evolving and modernising society. It also seems like a sink of corruption. We have only to recall that quite a few honorary policemen were vintners by profession, that it was the police who distributed licences to sell spirituous liqueurs, and that there were 500 licensed premises[7] for a population 30,000 (one for every 60 persons, or every 30 adults), to understand the possibilities.

And yet the very frequency with which licences were granted must have reduced the value of each one. If there really was one licence for every 30 adults, each one could not have been worth very much. The possibilities for corruption are far greater where licences are few and correspondingly valuable. The vast majority of licences granted in Jersey must have been to individuals of very modest means; by contrast, licensed premises these days belong mainly to giant brewery companies, with the means easily to influence those who grant licenses. I have no proof, but it seems to me likely that the decision to extend licensing hours throughout Great Britain, with the results that can be seen throughout the country, was influenced by the brewery companies. The corruption in 19th century Jersey was therefore as amateur as its policing.

Professionalisation of policing does not in the least, by itself, reduce corruption, for two reasons. First, the professionals are rarely paid enough to put them beyond the temptation to accept bribes, even small ones; second, because in any case man is a fallen creature and permanently in danger of temptation. It would be too much to say that every man has his price; but it would not be an exaggeration to say that many men have their price.

Nor does professionalisation, by itself, conduce to efficiency. Where bureaucracy increases to a certain point, efficiency declines and the ostensible purpose of an organisation ceases to be its real one: for the bureaucracy's interest is in increasing, not in solving, problems. Professionalisation often leads to intellectual corruption. Would anyone dare to aver that such a process had not undermined the British police?[8]

The impression I gained overall from researching the three murders was of a society with a strong and in many respects attractive flavour, with much more personal freedom than in our own. Perhaps it is distance and unfamiliarity that lends it so strong a flavour, for a way of life always seems savourless to those who actually live it and take it for granted as the only possible way to live. In one and a half centuries' time, perhaps our life will seem as exotic and interesting to those who feel that their own lives are without interest as the life of Victorian Jersey now seems to me to have been. And my cast of characters was hardly representative of the population as a whole.

What is quite clear, however, is that people in 19th century Jersey did not fear to speak their mind on public matters, as many people do today. There was not the undercurrent of fear of being thought beyond the pale of acceptable opinion (the pale of settlement of such opinion becoming ever narrower in extent); self-censorship about public questions appears to have been very slight. No doubt there is a law of conservation of self-censorship, inscribed in the nature of human society: and if the need for it does not attach to one thing, it will attach to another. Despite their uninhibited criticism of each other, Victorian Jerseymen were clearly genteel in their use of language, avoiding vulgar expressions even while indulging in insult. By the standard of an average conversation between young people to be overheard in the streets of Britain today, even Madame Le Gendre's expletives seem very mild, though even their use was regarded as evidence of her bad character.

There was another sense in which 19th century Jersey was a much freer society than ours: government and officialdom weighed very little in the lives of the citizens. The society seems to have been largely self-regulating, but it was not therefore chaotic.

The lack of regulation entailed risks: a man and his son made fireworks on premises in which common-sense suggests that they should not have been made, but there was no one to stop them, and as a result an old man lost his life. But, as Tocqueville said, he who seeks in liberty anything other than liberty itself (for example, safety from explosions in nearby firework factories) is destined for tyranny. This is not the same as saying that liberty is the only human *desideratum*; none of us actually does want to be blown up by a neighbour's firework manufactory. But it is well to recognise that the cost of safety is a loss of liberty, and to make a conscious choice between them, rather than go on pretending that the two are perfectly compatible and that, to adapt the pernicious title of a best-selling book, we can have it all.

Of course, life was much more precarious then than now, and in many respects very much harder. It was less abundant materially, and choice was much more limited; but it is possible that a less abundant life also means a life lived more intensely, though not more comfortably. People who lived in a single room were almost forced by circumstances into a vigorous social life, and at the very least did not have to spend much of their time on their own domestic arrangements, the upkeep of our possessions now taking a great deal of our time and energy. Richer people, of course, had servants, those great facilitators of ease of social intercourse.[9] And in an age of mass production, many of us scarcely take any notice of our own possessions, taking them for granted, they being all too easily replaceable at inconsiderable expense. When Jean René De La Croix was accused of receiving for resale a stolen pick into his bric-à-brac shop, it was because someone recognised it as belonging to someone else: that is to say, the pick had individuality which others had noticed. Many people now possess practically nothing that has such individuality, and as a result take much less detailed notice of the world around them. Their lives are lived on a broader scale, perhaps, but not on a deeper one.

Throughout my researches into the three murders in Jersey between December 1845 and February 1846 I wondered whether they served any purpose other than the narrow one of amusing me. The circumstances were that my wife, also a doctor, had taken a position as *locum tenens* in Jersey; and, as usual, I accompanied her. Clearly, I needed something to do, and it was then that the *main coupable* written on the tomb of M. Le Cronier happened to attract my attention. But the study of the past has long interested me, and I have always had an unformed and inchoate belief or intuition that it was of deep significance for mankind. How this belief came to me I cannot say, any more than I can say at what age (except that it was quite early in my life) I learnt that they spoke Portuguese in Brazil.[10] Once, when someone asked me what the study of history was *for* I found myself in the embarrassing position of asserting *that* it was important but of not being able to say quite *why* it was important.

I have since thought of reasons, apart from the intrinsic interest or fascination of the subject matter itself (and, after all, there must be ends in themselves if human life is to be liveable, and therefore things that are interesting in and for themselves, even without utilitarian value). These arguments are not sufficiently strong, perhaps, to change the mind of a man who thinks that history is bunk, but they give some form to my intuition. And what would our world be like if no one at all were interested in the past?

If human life is to have any significance beyond an eternal but constantly fleeting present moment, the past must be significant to us: for what is the present but the past of the future? Why should anyone who does not care for the past care for the future? Indeed, the feeling that life has no transcendent significance, that the present moment is all, is, in my view, one of the causes of much of our social pathology. For if the present moment is all that there is, it is necessary to make it as sensational or dramatic as possible – for man craves drama much more than he craves happiness.[11] Human life is thus lived as a succession of moments rather than as a biography, and even a man's own past ceases to have any significance or interest for him. It is not even a source of experience for him from which to learn or adapt; he lives his disasters as if they were not connected to or predictable from his own conduct.

Furthermore, all judgment is comparative, and history is one of the grand comparators available to mankind. If we do not appreciate that our present world is the result of development, we take everything for granted, as if it had always been there and always will be there. We think that the way we do things is the *only* way to do things, and this leads either to despair or to complacency, according to our assessment of our current situation. We have nothing to be grateful for and nothing to defend.

It is a curious aspect of a society given to multiculturalism almost as an official doctrine that fewer people seem to exhibit a genuine interest in the way that other people live and see, or once lived and saw, the world.[12] The past is indeed another country, where they do things differently; but at the same time, studying it allows us to appreciate that the existential dilemmas of human existence remain much the same, despite great variations in social arrangements and technological capacity, that man is a problem-creating animal as much as a problem-solving one, and that dissatisfaction is the permanent condition of mankind. This realisation might help us to put our own miseries and frustrations into some kind of perspective, and thereby help to reduce them. It promotes an ironical and civilised understanding of life.

The government and inhabitants of Jersey, and the intellectuals who interpreted reality for them, had to decide whether or not to reform the criminal law of Jersey behind a veil of ignorance. They neither knew what would happen if they reformed it nor what would happen if they failed to reform it; certainly, it never occurred to the reformers, not even once (for it never does), that they might make things worse as well as better.

In fact, ignorance is a permanent feature of human life, its glory and its burden. We are always leaping blindly into the future, having no choice but to do so, using whatever imperfect knowledge we may have available to guide us, for lack of anything better. The study of history might teach us to distinguish what is permanent in the human condition from what is adventitious in our particular situation: a knowledge that might render us suitably modest. Perhaps we should make our leaps into the future little reversible hops rather than irreversible running jumps.

Endnotes

Introduction

1 A *centenier* was a voluntary policemen in one of the 12 parishes of Jersey originally with 100 households under his jurisdiction, hence the name. His superior was the *connétable*, who was also a volunteer. They were elective positions, as they still are.

2 The then population of Jersey, though Shebbeare states a few pages later that it was 26,000.

3 John Shebbeare, *An Authentic Narrative of the Oppressions of the Islanders of Jersey, to which is prefixedA Succinct History of the Military, Actions, Constitution, Laws, Customs and Commerce of that Island*, S. Hooper, London, 1771.

4 The name for natives of Jersey.

Chapter I

1 *Chronique de Jersey*, 25 February, 1846.

2 *Chronique de Jersey*, 15 April, 1846.

3 *Chronique de Jersey*, 17 January 1846.

4 The Jersey census of 1841 gave the population as 47,556, and that of 1851 as 57,020.

5 He was the only policeman ever to have been killed in the line of duty in Jersey.

6 *Chronique de Jersey*, 17 December, 1845.

7 *Chronique de Jersey*, 17 January, 1846.

8 *Chronique de Jersey*, 28 January, 1846.

9 *Ibid.*

10 Reported in the *Chronique de Jersey*, 24 January, 1846.

11 Mrs Georgia Le Maistre.

12 *L'Impartial*, 3 December, 1845.

13 *Chronique de Jersey*, 24 December, 1845.

14 *Chronique de Jersey*, 18 February, 1846.

15 *Chronique de Jersey*, 25 February, 1846.

16 Then, as now, one of the principal shopping streets of St Helier.

17 *Chronique de Jersey*, 3 December, 1845.
18 *Chronique de Jersey*, 14 January, 1846.

Chapter II

1 *Ibid*
2 Major Pierson was killed in the Battle of Jersey, and it is his death that is the subject of John Singleton Copley's painting, now in the Tate Gallery.
3 *Chronique de Jersey*, 14 January, 1846.
4 *Chronique de Jersey*, 28 January, 1846.
5 *Chronique de Jersey*, 14 January, 1846.
6 *Ibid.*
7 *Chronique de Jersey*, 28 January 1846.
8 *Chronique de Jersey*, 21 February 1846.
9 *Ibid.*
10 *Ibid.*
11 *Chronique de Jersey*, 1 April, 1846.
12 *Chronique de Jersey*, 8 April, 1846.
13 *Chronique de Jersey*, 11 April, 1846.
14 *Stewards of the Media: A Jersey History*, p. 14, Roy McLaughlin, Société Jersiaise, 1999.
15 *The Newspaper Press Directory*, Charles Mitchell, 1846. This publication lists seven journals published on the island, but since it fails to mention the *Chronique de Jersey*, there must have been at least eight, and possibly more if there were other omissions. It states that *Le Constitutionnel* had the largest circulation of any French-language journal on the island.

Chapter III

1 In English in the original, *Chronique de Jersey*, 18 February, 1846.
2 *Chronique de Jersey*, 25 February 1846.
3 In English in the original.
4 *Chronique de Jersey*, 18 March, 1846.

Chapter IV

1 *A Biographical Dictionary of Jersey*, G R Balleine, London, Staples Press, 1948.

2 For some reason, practically none of the early English-language press of Jersey survives. No more than a few isolated copies are known. Much of the French-language press of the same era survives.

3 *On the Philosophy of a Diving Revelation*, Abraham Le Cras, Jersey, 1844, p. 1.

4 *Ibid.*, p. 9.

5 *The Triumph of the Country: the Rural Community in Nineteenth Century Jersey*, John C Kelleher, John Appleby Publishing and la Société Jersiaise, 2nd Ed. 1995, pp 136-167.

6 *Ibid.*

7 A few elderly people still speak it today, but no young people as a native language. It all but has died out, though there are attempts to revive it in schools. Small as Jersey is, there was more than one dialect of it, an indication of how restricted geographically the lives of rural people could be not so very long ago.

8 See the Correspondence book of Abraham Jones Le Cras, Jersey Archives, D/2/J/A1.

9 See, for example, Beyond Reason: Art and Psychosis Works from the Prinzhorn Collection, Hayward Gallery, 1996.

10 See Correspondence book Abraham Jones Le Cras, Jersey Archives, D/2/JA1.

11 *L'Impartial*, 3 December, 1845.

12 *Chronique de Jersey*, 24 October, 1846.

13 Abraham Jones Le Cras, op. cit.

14 *Minutes of Evidence taken before the Commissioners for Enquiring into the State of the Criminal Law in the Channel Islands*, 1846, pp 127-8.

15 *Ibid.*, p. 129.

16 *Ibid.* p. 133.

17 *Ibid.* pp 169-70.

18 *Ibid.*

Chapter V

1 *Le Constitutionnel*, 7 March, 1846.

2 *Ibid.* pp. 206-9.

3 The historian, Roy Porter, mentions the connection between newspaper ownership and patent medicine-selling in his book, *Quacks: Fakers and Charlatans in English Medicine*, 2nd Ed. 2000,pp 109 – 112, but even he does not make clear quite how close the relationship was.

4 Is there no *balm in Gilead*? Is there no physician there? Why then is not the health of the daughter of my people recovered? Jeremiah 8:22.

Chapter VI

1 Victor Hugo, *L'Archipel de la Manche.*

2 William Davies, *Fort Regent; a History*, Jersey, privately printed, 1971.

3 Nicholas Le Cornu, *Les maisons de débauche et maisons malfamées: Brothels and Houses of Ill-fame in Jersey, 1790 – 1918,* Bulletin of the Jersey Society in London, March 2001, pp 9-11.

4 *Ibid.*

5 *Le Constitutionnel*, 21 March, 1846.

6 Le Cornu, *op. cit.*

Chapter VII

1 This appears as *b......d* in the original. The word *bugger* and its cognates were apparently much in use as vulgar expressions in Jersey of the time.

2 There, there, my girl, you wouldn't want to do that.

3 *b.....e* in the original report in the *Chronique de Jersey* of 22 April, 1846.

4 Suggesting that it was not difficult to find candidates for the post of prostitute.

5 Presumably *bastard* or *bugger*. Bastard was the worse insult.

6 In English at the trial. Whether M. Manuel was guilty of

cowardice, or merely exercising prudence, by fleeing before the knife-wielding Madame Le Gendre, and leaving his superior, M. Le Cronier, in Mulberry Cottage, is a question that is not easy to answer. In any case, while one can *praise* exceptional bravery, one cannot *demand* it.

Chapter VIII

1 This is not as mean as it might at first appear. Under Jersey law, a man was obliged to leave a third of his estate to his wife, and a third to his children (if any). This applied to Le Cronier, who had a wife and children. A man was then free to bequeath the final third of his estate to whomever he chose. Therefore Le Cronier chose to leave the maximum permitted to his wife. *'L'homme marié qui a des enfants ou des descendents conserve un droit de disposition qui est fixé a un tiers.'* See Charles Sydney Le Gros, *Traité du droit coutumier de l'ile de Jersey*, p. 126, Jersey and Guernsey Law Review, 2007.

2 Dr Joseph Dickson was later to distinguish himself by getting up a petition to have Victor Hugo, who was then a political refugee on Jersey from the regime of Louis Napoleon, expelled from the island. Hugo was believed by his enemies to have insulted Queen Victoria, and to be a general troublemaker. Hugo was expelled; he left Jersey and went to live in Guernsey, a different jurisdiction. See *Letter to His Excellency Major-General Love, Lieut. Governor of the Island of Jersey, Disputing his Pretended Right to Expel Strangers from the Island,* by someone calling himself *Justicia*, St Helier, 1856.

3 D/Y/A/26/52.

4 It was assumed that men would not lie in these circumstances.

Chapter IX

1 http://www.policememorial.org.uk/Forces/StatesofJersey/Jersey_Roll.htm.

2 According to Sir John Le Couteur's diary, there were 20,000 mourners, that is to say more than 40 per cent of the population of the island.

3 *La lyre exilée*, L. D. Hurel, Jersey, 1847, p. 199.

4 *Dictionary of Painters of the Channel Islands*, Philip Stevens, JAB Publsihing, Jersey, 2002.

5 Mrs Patricia Neale, personal information.

6 One should also remember the poverty of the population by comparison with today's.

7 Which, nevertheless, is more than that left by the great majority of people.

8 I owe this information to Mrs Anna Baghiani.

9 *Le général de Gaulle est mort. La France est veuve* (General de Gaulle is dead. France is a widow). Thus President Pompidou on the death of the General.

10 He dies murdered! Before this frightful crime,/ this terror, horror, odious, impious monster!/ You did not retreat… day forever fatal! /Day of eternal grief! towards the celestial vault/ Only sad gazes are raised, distraught! / Cry! people! cry! GEORGE CRONIER is no more! And (in the mouth of Madame Le Cronier): He dies! he is no more! Unhappy wife!/ It would be better that I had never been born./ On this earth, alas, what have I to do now?/ Cruel gods! Take back your present!/ You are no more! dear husband! what is life to me!/ You are no more! my happiness is destroyed for ever…

Chapter X

1 In the account in *Le Constitutionnel*, March 25, 1846, the word *bugger* is both capitalised and printed in full, by comparison with the semantic delicacy of the *Chronique de Jersey*. As the *Journal du bien public* it no doubt considered this frankness sane and healthy.

2 M. Le Chevalier did not specify what books he had in mind, other than the Bible.

3 *Chronique de Jersey*, 22 April, 1846, and *Le Constitutionnel*, 25 April, 1846. The papers, although bitterly opposed to one another, had virtually the same account of the trial, suggesting that they used an official transcript. The difference in date was because the *Chronique* was twice weekly, the *Constitutionnel* once.

4 *Chronique de Jersey*, 4 March 1846.

Chapter XI

1 Hammond (1801 – 1880) gave more evidence to the Royal Commission of 1846 than any other person. He studied Norman law at Caen, was appointed Bailiff in 1858, and died on the bench while delivering a judgment. According to *A Biographical Dictionary of Jersey*, his one weakness was snuff-taking; he once adjourned a trial while some was procured for him. He was the grandfather of the famous social historian, John Hammond.

2 In English in the original.

3 In English in the original.

4 Sir William Blackstone (1723 – 1780), English judge and academic lawyer, whose *Commentaries on the Laws of England* went through many editions, and tried to extract the principles underlying English law.

5 In English in the original.

6 The last wars to have affected the island being the Napoleonic wars.

7 In English in the original.

8 In English in the original.

9 In English in the original.

10 Matthew Hale (1609 – 1676), judge and jurist who strongly influenced Blackstone.

11 In English in the original.

Chapter XII

1 People with front teeth missing who are not otherwise edentulous have almost always lost them violently, either in sporting accidents or, more usually, in brawls. Brawls are not distributed randomly among the population.

2 *Le Constitutionnel*, 22 April, 1837.

3 *Regulations for the Prison and House of Correction in Jersey*, 1845.

Chapter XIII

1 Now, of course, Tasmania.

2 Mary Phillips, File MP 105, Lord Coutanche Library, *Société Jersiaise.*

3 http://www.capitalpunishmentuk.org/islands.html.

4 *Report from the Select Committee of the House of Lords, appointed to "Take into Consideration the present Mode of carrying into effect CAPITAL PUNISHMENTS,"* 17 July 1856.

5 Dr Johnson, a humane man, was famously – or notoriously - in favour of executions in public. The death penalty failed of its deterrent effect, he thought, if it was carried out away from the public gaze. In this, great man as he was, he was almost certainly mistaken.

6 What use is it to you to order an odious demise?/ You frighten in vain: you do not correct.

7 But an example is needed… What! Has the horrible appearance of a bloody scaffold/

Ever changed the heart of a criminal engaged in crime?/ No; this hideous drama, this

Terrible spectacle,/ Is a fine day for him; his heart likes it; it pleases him.

8 Do not listen at all to the wishes of the foaming crowd,/ Who, all too like the tiger, is avid for blood,/ Who, in order to see close up an infamous death,/ Take their place early in the first row.

9 The law recognises legitimate murders,/ But are these murders any the less crimes for it?/ In vain does humanity make its voice heard,/ The law forbids and orders murder at the same time.

10 Life is God's only; He holds I in His hands;/ He alone disposes of unhappy humans.

11 Your judgments have often struck down the innocent!/ How do you dare, then, without horror or fear,/ Pronounce the death sentence!

12 You order his death… but his children, his wife,/ You kill them also; it is to kill the innocent.

13 How beautiful and great it is! This august privilege/ Of snatching a poor condemned man from death…

14 More accurately a form of utilitarianism known as rule utilitarianism.

15 To encourage the others.

16 David Fraser, personal communication.

17 An assumption that, admittedly, might not be justified.

18 Unlike in Tsarist Russia which, at the time, was supposedly a model of cruelty and oppression.

19 He might then not have been able to do what he did, for purely physical reasons.

20 For confirmation, see *Drunken Comportment*, Craig McAndrew and Robert B Edgerton, Aldine Publishing, 1969, a classic work not superseded.

21 For the evidence, see Herbert Fingarette's book, *Heavy Drinking*, California University Press, 1988.

22 The law has changed in a more permissive, and less intelligent, direction recently.

23 A delusion shared, no doubt, by much of the population; and indeed a book by Professor Richard Moran, *Knowing Right from Wrong*, Free Press, 1981, suggests that M'Naghten *was* being followed and spied upon because of his political activities, and furthermore that he had been paid to assassinate Sir Robert Peel and appear mad afterwards in the event of being caught. Whether a man would consent to live the rest of his life – a further 22 years, M'Naghten dying in 1865 – between Bedlam and Broadmoor for the sake of such a cause, without ever revealing the truth, I rather doubt. In any case, I shall take M'Naghten's delusion at face value, that is to say as a *delusion*.

24 Or diminished responsibility.

25 *Chronique de Jersey*, 15 August, 1846.

Chapter XIV

1 No relation, as far as I am aware, to the Drs Dickson of Jersey.

2 Simpkin and Marshall, 1843.

3 Drummond was unlucky. He was shot a year or two before the discovery of anaesthetics.

4 Samuel Dickson, *What Killed Mr. Drummond, the Lead or the Lancet?*

5 Thomas Wakley was a stormy petrel. A campaigning editor, as well as coroner, his collected trials for libel would make an interesting – though quite lengthy – volume.

6 Except in cases of *polycythaemia rubra vera*, an uncommon condition in which too many red blood cells are produced, leading – untreated – to strokes and other pathological conditions. I remember as a young doctor periodically removing the blood of a patient with this condition. It was said that the blood thus removed was excellent food for roses, a claim that I did not investigate.

7 *Dictionary of National Biography*, 2006.

8 *The Detection of Secret Homicide*, John Havard, Macmillan, 1960, p xiii.

Chapter XV

1 *Chronique de Jersey*, 29 April, 1846.

2 *Chronique de Jersey*, 25 April, 1846.

3 Quoted in *Capital Punishment and British Politics*, James B. Christoph, Allen and Unwin, 1962, p. 16.

4 Letters *808.6 PER,p167, Lord Coutanche Library, Société Jersiaise.

5 *Ibid.*. pp 167-8.

6 *Ibid.* pp 168.

7 *Ibid.* p 168.

8 In fact, there was not to be another murder in Jersey for more than two years after Madame Le Gendre killed George Le Cronier. See Mary Phillips, MP105, Lord Coutanche Library, Société Jersiaise.

9 There is a possible analogy here with the introduction of television into a society that previously did not have it. Rates of violence do not increase immediately, but only ten or so years later, when those who have grown up with the evil screen reach the age at which, actuarially, they are most likely to commit acts of violence.

10 Heinemann Educational Books.

11 This is notwithstanding Arthur Koestler's remark, in his *Reflections on Hanging*, Gollancz, 1956, that 'Hanging is all right for Englishmen; they actually seem to like it.' This follows his discussion of the evidence of Albert Pierrepoint, the hangman, to the Royal Commission on Capital Punishment of 1949, namely

that he had had only one difficult condemned man – *client,* I
suppose we'd have to call him today – to hang, who 'was not an
Englishman, and he kicked up rough.' Mr Pierrepoint's evidence
was confirmed by the Under-Sheriff of London, Mr H.N. Gedge,
who said, 'He was a foreigner, and I have noticed that English
people take their punishment better than foreigners.'

12 And this is in fact what happened.

13 Of course, it is also possible that these desperate women do
indeed now resort to more violent methods. If the proportion
of murder-suicides had remained unchanged, despite a general
rise in the homicide rate, this would be an argument against the
deterrent effect of the death penalty.

14 Norman Mailer, *Advertisements for Myself,* André Deutsch, 1961,
p.299.

Chapter XVI

1 *Le Constitutionnel,* 23 May, 1846.

2 By which is meant most of the press apart from the present
journal.

3 Mount Sinister, the place of public executions in Jersey.

4 It was characteristic of the increasingly authoritarian nature
of British governments (combined, of course, with both laxity
and incompetence) that the last Labour government seriously
considered placing people under preventive detention *before they had
done anything illegal* if they were deemed by experts to be dangerous.
On the one hand, then, increasing leniency towards those who
had done something illegal, and increasing severity towards those
who *might* do something illegal: a logical extension, perhaps, of
Castigator's sensibility.

5 It is worth here comparing *Castigator's* argument with that of
Voltaire in his *Treatise on Toleration.* Voltaire protested against what
amounted to the judicial murder of Jean Calas, a Protestant
merchant of Toulouse, whose son committed suicide but who was
accused, without any evidence, of having killed him because he
had threatened to convert to Catholicism, and was executed in
the most cruel possible way. 'If the accused has no defence but

his virtue... if the judges can kill merely by decree, after a public outcry, everyone will fear for himself, and no one will be sure of his life...' This is an argument against arbitrariness, not the death penalty, in favour of the rule of law, not of leniency or of mercy.
6 They were ably deployed in the Report from the Select Committee of the House of Lords on Public Executions, 1856, that is to say only ten years later, a Report that led to the abolition of executions in public.

Chapter XVII

1 Letters *808.6 PER, p176, Lord Coutanche Library, Société Jersiaise.
2 *Ibid.* p. 175. The Reverend Perrot was quite mistaken in his estimate of the Royal Commission. It carried out its work with admirable thoroughness and integrity, and found that many, indeed most, of Le Cras' complaints, as well of those of *L'Impartial*, were fully justified. One of its two members, Thomas Flower Ellis, was an eminent barrister, and Lord Macaulay's closest, and very nearly inseparable, friend. I doubt that Lord Macaulay would have conferred this degree of friendship lightly, on an inconsiderable man. See the *Dictionary of National Biography*.
3 Jersey did a good trade in the re-export to Britain of French goods, which thereby avoided import duty. Apparently cows were imported from France, and exported as Jersey cattle. Oddly enough, there was manufacturing in Jersey, though the island had no natural advantages as a manufacturer, and several disadvantages. Imported wool was made into jerseys and exported to Britain. This was initially done to keep the population of Jersey, then deemed important strategically, in employment, and thereby prevent it from emigrating.
4 One is reminded, almost, of Marx's famous but fatuous description of Man under fully achieved communism, in his *The German Ideology*: 'In communist society, where nobody has one exclusive field of activity but each can become accomplished in any branch he wishes, society regulates the general production and thus makes it possible for me to do one thing today and another

tomorrow, to hunt in the morning, fish in the afternoon, rear cattle in the evening, criticise after dinner, just as I have a mind, without ever becoming hunter, fisherman, shepherd or critic.' If it is strange how potent cheap music is, it is even stranger how intelligent and even brilliant men can come to write, and believe, such patent drivel.

5 I once myself wrote a for-and-against article – under different names – in the same edition of a newspaper. This kind of exercise is no doubt good for one's powers of argumentation, though not necessarily for one's character. Perhaps it helps one to appreciate that there are two sides to every question.

6 *Le Constitutionnel* was a weekly.

7 To elect honorary policemen.

8 The fact that the relations of Arthur Koestler, quoted above, were of sadistic and even criminal violence, if David Cesarini's biography is to be believed, does not affect the validity, or otherwise, of his arguments in *Reflections on Hanging*.

9 *Le Constitutionnel*, 7 February, 1846.

10 It seems possible that taking a boat in order to carry on an illicit liaison is a continuing Jersey tradition. On returning to St Helier from St Malo, my wife and I saw parked outside the port a large 4x4 vehicle draped with a sheet upon which the words 'X. X. [name withheld by me] is a cheating slut' written on it in very large letters. A man in his forties was standing by the car, and apologised to us for the vulgarity of the language. 'But,' he said, 'it's my wife. I've just found out, and she's coming back from St Malo today.'

11 *La Chronique de Jersey*, Wednesday, 11 February, 1846.

12 Notwithstanding that it was a weekly publication.

13 If this is the criterion, almost every writer is an ignoramus. I notice, however, that notwithstanding his enmity towards the *Chronique*, Jean De La Croix took to heart its criticism, and in a future article used the word *bizarrerie* rather than his own *bizarrure*, a word of his own invention.

14 As the parliamentary assembly of the island is known.

This charge is borne out by an examination of the records of the hospital now in the Jersey Archive.

15 *La ville de St-Hélier, épisode historique d'une histoire inédite de Jersey,* Jersey, 1845, p. 180.

16 The government of Anthony Blair encouraged mass public drunkenness by pretending to think that, if alcohol were available all day round to the binge drinkers of Britain, they would start drinking in a more Latin fashion, that is to say sipping their *vin rosé* as an aperitif on the terraces of cafés while holding conversations about life and literature. I suspect that one day research will prove a rather more sordid motive for its obviously deleterious policy. I am by no means a Marxist, and do not believe in the economic explanation of everything; but in this case, I would suggest a shortcut to future researchers: *cherchez l'argent!*

17 Sue's novel, once immensely popular, is to a modern sensibility prolix, implausible, melodramatic, in short unreadable. Here, however, is the description of Rodin as he first appears in the book:

18 Fifty years of age, he wore an old, threadbare, olive-coloured, long-tailed coat, with a greasy collar; a pocket-handkerchief was his cravat, with waistcoat and trowsers of black cloth, worn white at the seams and knees; whilst his feet plunged in shoes of oiled leather, rested on a small green-baize stool, which was on the red and shining floor. His gray hairs fell limp and flat on his temples, and crowned his bald forehead; his eyebrows were scarcely marked; his upper eyelid shrivelled, but falling low, like the membrane of a reptile's eye, half-concealed his small and sharp black eye; his lips, thin and absolutely colourless, were lost in the wan hue of his lank visage, his peaked nose, and peaked chin. This livid and (it might almost be said) *lipless* mask seemed the more strange from its death-like inanimation, and but for the rapid motion of M. Rodin's fingers as he stooped over his bureau, and his pen scratched along, he might have been taken for a corpse. Eugene Sue, *The Wandering Jew,* Chapman and Hall, 1844, vol. 1, chapter XV, p. 96.

19 I have not been able to trace the episode to which this example of venality refers.

20 Perhaps he means *menteur,* liar.

21 He who had arrested the editor for beating his wife.

22 Wm. Baker was put in the dock by M. *le Centenier* Le Cronier,
accused of having stolen a shirt and a pair of shoes. The accused
subsequently sold the shirt for a shilling to M. Jean de la Croix,
who has a little second-hand shop at the bottom of Bath Street...
L'Impartial, 22 October, 1845. It must be an occupational hazard
of dealers in second-hand goods that they buy stolen goods from
time to time. The fact that such goods are sold at a low price, a
fraction of their true value, is not in itself evidence either, for those
who resort to selling their belongings are often desperate and will
take whatever they can get. Dealers must surely know this and
take advantage of it. It is the operation of the market place.

23 I have not been able to trace who these might be, or from what
public posts they were removed. It cannot mean the disappointed
candidates for police positions, because they were honorary, and
it was the view of the *Chronique* that, the system being perfect and
needing no reform, they were not used for personal enrichment.

24 *Chronique de Jersey*, 29 July, 1846.

Chapter XVIII

1 *Le Constitutionnel*, 17 January, 1846.

2 For most crimes, *mens rea* – a guilty mind – is a necessary
precondition of a criminal act having been committed at all. A
man who acts in a state of post-ictal (epileptic) automatism, for
example, is not guilty of a crime. As St Augustine put it, if one
does not sin by will, one does not sin.

3 *The Theory of Moral Sentiments*, Chapter 1.

4 David Fraser, author of *Badlands: NZ, A Land Fit for Criminals*,
2011, performed a regression analysis of the crime rates of 97
countries, and showed that the crime rate was not only higher in
richer countries, but higher in those countries with less inequality,
although this correlation between crime and equality just failed to
reach the level of statistical significance. In *The Growth of* Crime,
published in 1977, the criminologists Sir Leon Radzinowicz and
Joan King wrote that 'Through the years of economic upheaval,
unemployment and another great war, [crime] gathered pace
inexorably... as the curve of affluence was gathering momentum,

the curve of crime began to follow it.' So both poverty and affluence are, at the least, associated with, and possibly cause, crime. Never mind: the search for exculpatory explanation – other than the nature of Man or Original Sin – must go on.

5 It is strange, and further evidence of the desire, widespread among intellectuals at least, to find exculpatory explanations for criminal acts, that it is always the criminal's conduct that is held to be determined by circumstances and never that of the judge who sentences him to punishment. It is useless to protest – useless, that is, philosophically, though perhaps not useless rhetorically or in practice – that the criminal's behaviour is determined, and that therefore punishment is unjust because he could have done no other; for the conduct of those who punish him must also, *ex hypothesi*, be likewise determined, and they could do no other than to punish him. A fully consistent determinism would leave everything as it was. That is why the English law is quite right in holding that a man is responsible for his actions unless it can be proved, on the balance of probability, that he was not: for thoroughgoing determinism is either too lenient or too severe in its consequences.

6 *The Eighteenth Brumaire of Louis Bonaparte.*

7 In explaining human motivation, it is difficult not to resort to the *ad hominem*. The attempt to do so frequently results in the inhuman.

8 www.merseyside.police.uk/index.aspx?/articleid=10439.

Chapter XIX

1 Their private employment by citizens was an implicit reproach to the police, whose protection against criminals was felt by those who employed them to be inadequate.

2 The same defence might be made of the police in the recent (2011) riots in London. The police were accused by some of letting the rioters run riot without attempting to stop them by force. But inadequate force only increases violence and the risk of death or serious injury. I know from my experience as a prison doctor that the last impression you want to give a disorderly criminal is that he

might win a contest of strength.

3 No copies exist of this newspaper contemporary to the crime.

4 According to Schopenhauer, it always is.

5 The article that allegedly Madame Le Gendre had been reading shortly before she killed M. Le Cronier.

6 ie the assault on Le Cras.

7 It is one that has recently touched me personally. The Norwegian mass-murderer, Anders Breivik, cited me indirectly in his 1500-page rant, written before he murdered 86 people. It goes without saying (I hope) that nothing I have ever written could be taken by any reasonable man as an incitement to murder.

8 *Le Constitutionnel*, 24 January 1846.

9 In English in the original.

10 *Le Constitutionnel*, 24 October, 1846.

11 This was actually the response of a Chief Constable to an article I wrote complaining of the failure of the police to arrest people who committed crimes before their very eyes.

Chapter XX

1 *Le Constitutionnel*, 28 March, 1846.

2 *Chronique de Jersey*, 17 December, 1845.

3 It was different in the case of Thomas Nicolle: *his* resort to the Bible was deemed sincere. 'We learn,' wrote the *Chronique* of 25 March, 1846, 'that Thomas Nicolle realises his painful situation, and actively applies himself to the work of repentance. The prisoner shows himself sensible of all the consolations that the ministers of religion bring... He passes his time in reading the Word of God, expresses his regrets at having so long neglected it, and says that he draws great consolation from it.' How does one tell that Le Gendre was bogus while Nicolle was sincere? Who can see into men's souls? Part of the answer must surely lie in the consistency of the behaviour; Madame Le Gendre's moods and conduct changed like the weather in April. Of course it is possible that at each individual moment she was sincere.

4 Contrary to the implication in the newspapers, this outbreak of emotion at a relatively neutral moment in the proceedings

is not a sign of insincerity. People do not always break down at the 'appropriate', which is to say expected, moments of the proceedings.

5 *Le Constitutionnel*, 30 May, 1846.

6 I do not know of what crime he had been found guilty.

7 *Chronique de Jersey*, 15 August, 1846.

8 *Ibid.* In the event, Thomas Nicolle was transported to Tasmania.

9 *Le Constitutionnel*, 28 February, 1846.

10 *She Must Have Known*, Geoffrey Wansell.

11 The name Bridget Brown appears among the prostitutes who were admitted to the General Hospital in 1849. The Bridget Brown admitted to the hospital gave her age as 23, but the Bridget Brown whom Pierre Le Gendre attacked was 15 or 16, and so would have been 19 at the most in 1849. It is possible that she gave a false age to make herself appear more adult than she was; or that it was a different Bridget Brown. Three other Browns were admitted to the hospital as prostitutes, Caroline (twice), Jane and Betsey. Betsey (Elizabeth) may well have been Bridget's sister. According to the census of 1841, a family of the name of Brown lived in the Great Union Road, near a pub called the Cross Keys (today the Great Union). The family then consisted of John, aged 55, English, who was or had been a soldier, his Irish wife Julia aged 45, and four daughters, Mary Ann, 20, Elizabeth, 15, Bridget, 10 and Sarah, 7. Bridget aged 10 would have been 15 or 16 when Pierre-Marie Le Gendre attacked her. The age of Elizabeth fits that of Betsey, the prostitute admitted to the hospital in 1849. Would the Brown parents have known that two of their daughters were prostitutes? Would they have cared, or been resigned to it, would they have approved or disapproved of it?

12 The article does not state whether she went to the hospital for medical or moral reasons. The latter is more likely; after all, no one suggested for a moment that *Centenier* Le Cronier should go to hospital for treatment of what was a far more serious wound. It is true that there is a report of Bridget Brown's discharge from hospital, her wound 'healed,' but it does not follow that she was admitted that this wound might heal.

13 A study was once performed of those people who had survived throwing themselves from high buildings with intent to commit suicide. About half of them change their minds halfway down and regretted what they had done. But one wouldn't say as a consequence that they had never really intended to kill themselves in the first place.

Chapter XXI

1 *Le Miroir*, 23 May, 1846.

2 *Ibid.*

3 www.jerseyheritage.org/media/PDFs/Crime%20and%20 Punishment.pdf. This website is not wholly reliable. It states, for example, that once in Tasmania Madame Le Gendre remarried a man called Le Cronier *ie* the same name as that of her victim. This is not true, but I have traced the legend as far back as 1950, when such a claim was made in a Jersey newspaper by a local historian called Philip Ahier. Whether he himself was misled, or he made up the story of whole cloth, I do not know; but it is an interesting small instance of how an untruth may be propagated and become accepted as the truth.

4 www.capitalpunishment.uk.org/islands/html.

5 Mary Phillips, *op. cit.*

6 I am not sure, however, in what percentage of cases the murder was solved. It was likely to be very high. Social and geographical conditions in Jersey were not conducive to successful concealment. In psychological theory, inconsistent reward – if hanging may be regarded as a reward – is more effective in its conditioning effect than consistent reward

7 Assuming an equal distribution throughout the century, which as we shall see is not quite accurate.

8 The former Prime Minister, Mr Brown, claimed to be happier with figures than with people. It turned out that he wasn't very good at the former, either.

Chapter XXII

1 *Sydney Morning Herald*, 12 February, 1844.

Chapter XXIII

1 'The beer went mad, doctor,' was a frequent locution among my patients.

2 On Thomas Nicolle, see *Archives Office of Tasmania CON/33/1/84 Pestongee Bomangee.*

3 I have never subscribed to the mystical doctrine that the greater the sinner, the greater – subsequently – the saint. Nor do I think that the wish or intention to become a saint later on in life gives *carte blanche* to current conduct.

Chapter XXIV

1 *Founders & Survivors: Australian life course in historical context 1803 – 1920.* Also *Archives Office of Tasmania CON41/1/11 Conduct of Female Convicts arriving in the Period of the Probation system 1st Jan 1844 – 31st Dec 1853.*

2 Though, in my experience, women's prisons are worse than men's for aggression and violence. Perhaps this is because the criminal threshold for sending women to prison is generally higher than for men. Such gallantry on the part of the criminal justice system generally goes unremarked. Few, at any rate, are the feminists who call for an equalisation of the sex-ratio in the prison population, though this might, of course, be just as well achieved by letting male prisoners out as by imprisoning more females.

3 It is curious how often people promote or discover things just at the wrong moment. In the year before the discovery of anaesthesia, there was a spate of books describing the use of hypnosis to produce painless surgery.

4 See *Creating Born Criminals*, Nicole Hahn Rafter, University of Illinois Press, 1997, p. 120. Interestingly, when I turned to Lombroso himself, in the edition I have of his *L'Uomo delinquente*, 2nd French edition (L'Homme criminel), 1887, I found that, at least

then, he did *not* emphasise a low or sloping brow. 'I do not find, either, that there is a clear difference [between criminals and the delightfully named 'honest people'] in the frontal index' (p155). Indeed, he found, on examining 383 skulls of criminals, that only 8.6 per cent of them had small or narrow foreheads, as against 58.2 per cent of them who had prominent supraorbital ridges, the bony prominence over which lie the eyebrows (p. 165).

5 The Tasmanian records were obtained and transcribed for me by Mrs Baghiani. See also http://search.archives.tas.gov.au/ImageViewer/imageviewer.htm?CON15-1-4,374,22,F,56.

6 The most notorious and brutal of murderers, especially of women, rarely go without offers of marriage from women they have never met, sight unseen. Lesser criminals – recidivist shoplifters, for example – receive no such offers. On this subject, and the outcome of such 'affairs', see *Dream Lovers*, Jaquelynne Willcox-Bailey, Sydney, 2000.

7 I am grateful to Jeremy Palmer, of Anzestry, New South Wales, for this information.

8 Mrs Baghiani, personal communication.

Chapter XXV

1 Even when one makes an adjustment for the increased population before and after 1853, the difference is not statistically significant.

2 A comparison of the rates of miscarriage of justice between then and now would be highly instructive, if rather difficult to carry out. Of course, our current delay in trying alleged murderers might be caused by a higher ratio of such crimes to the number of lawyers necessary to try them than existed in Victorian times. That is not my impression, I must confess; and it has sometimes occurred to me that an expansion in the number of criminal lawyers – that is to say, lawyers who practise in the criminal courts, not lawyers who commit crimes – has actually created a demand for crime, which accounts for the leniency with which recidivists are treated in Great Britain. The lawyers *need* recidivists as shopkeepers need customers.

3 In the famous, or infamous, Bywaters and Thompson case of the early 1920s, Mrs Thompson would almost certainly not have been found guilty had she not insisted on going into the witness box. Her gross error of judgment, against the advice of her great defence advocate, Sir Henry Curtis Bennett, did not mean that her execution was nevertheless *not* a terrible and shameful miscarriage of justice.

4 Pardoned, *not* forgiven.

5 Of course, strictly speaking they were not murderers.

6 I have worked this out from the figures given in *A Brief History of Crime*, Peter Hitchens.

Chapter XXVI

1 At one time I had hoped to find evidence that she had returned to her old business in Tasmania, but none was forthcoming, and what would have been a good, or sensational, story was ruined. Now I am glad that I found no such evidence. I would much prefer that she really did regret what she had done, as being more creditable to the human race.

2 I attend such trials as an expert witness from time to time.

3 Among other derogations of the rule of law. For example, they suggested that the legal definition of a racist incident should be an incident that anyone, participant or observer, thought was racist. They did not consider that there should be any requirement that such a thought should be reasonable, or in accord with any objective fact. That a British judge could put his name to so sinister a suggestion shows that, far from our self-conception ('It couldn't happen here'), we are not very far removed from totalitarianism. The same authors suggested that conversations in private, if racist, should fall under the purview of the criminal law. See the MacPherson report into the killing of Stephen Lawrence.

4 Nowadays, Jerseymen and residents of the island refer to the UK as a foreign country. While much about Jersey is culturally familiar to other Britons, it uses the pound sterling as its currency, and Jerseymen consider themselves British, Jersey is genuinely foreign in other respects. It is not part of the European Union,

for example; one passes through customs on arrival there from the UK. Above all, it has no government debt.

5 It died out, more or less, with the appearance in 1959 of the last volume of the *Great British Trials* series of William Hodge and Company, a series containing eighty-four volumes that had been published for more than fifty years. I know of no richer reading. The introductions by their editors were almost always in exemplary prose. I am glad to say that an English murder trial is still by far the best free theatre in the world.

6 See, for example, *The Strange Death of Moral Britain*, Christie Davies, and *A Brief History of Crime*, Peter Hitchens.

7 According to Abraham Jones Le Cras, who may have been exaggerating for rhetorical purposes, though I think we can take it that he must have cited a credible number, within at least spitting distance of the correct one.

8 See, for example, PC Copperfield's *Wasting Police Time* and Inspector Gadget's *Perverting the Course of Justice*, both Monday Books.

9 The economist Joseph Schumpeter once said that a single servant was worth a household full of appliances. Anyone who has lived with servants knows this to be true. The question is why so many of us should feel so uncomfortable with this truth? We are not made nearly so uncomfortable by the contemplation of mass chronic unemployment.

10 Unlike, say, Mr Blair, our former Prime Minister, who apparently learned it only after he became Prime Minister.

11 Once when I worked in some remote Pacific islands I discovered that certain young people were sniffing petrol fumes. The effects of this were principally nausea, headache and dizziness, not effects that anyone, you might suppose, would wish to produce in himself. When asked why they did it, they replied that it was the *change* of mental state that they valued, not the quality of mental state produced by that change. They lived on islands where the day was always exactly 12 hours long and the temperature hardly varied by more than a few degrees.

12 An example of the narrowing of mental horizons that has occurred *pari passu* with the advancement of multiculturalism as

a doctrine is the following. Once, when I travelled to a remote country, a publication for which I have written for many years would take an article from me because 'No one knows anything about it.' Some years ago, it started to refuse to take an article from me on precisely the same grounds, namely that 'No one knows anything about it.' Whether this represented a narrowing of the horizons of the editors or the reading public, or of both, I am not sure; but it results in a narrowing.

Second Opinion: A Doctor's Dispatches from the Inner City
Theodore Dalrymple (hdbk, £14.99)

THEODORE DALRYMPLE has spent much of his working life as a doctor in a grim inner city hospital and the nearby prison; his patients are drug addicts and drunks, violent men and battered women, suicidal teenagers and despairing elderly. For many years, Dalrymple - acknowledged as the world's leading doctor-writer - wrote a column in The Spectator in which he recounted his experiences. This collection of those shocking, amusing and elegant columns offers a window into a world many of us never see.

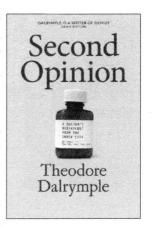

'The harsh truths he tells are all the more shocking because the media, in general, is unwilling to tell them' - *Daily Telegraph*

'He actually cares about the people at the bottom of the social heap while public sector jobsworths and slimy politicians only pretend to' - *Daily Express*

'A rare voice of truth' - *The Spectator*

'He could not be further from the stereotype of the "little Englander" conservative... he is arguably our greatest living essayist' - *Standpoint*

From all good bookshops, online from www.mondaybooks.com or via 01455 221752. All of our titles are also available as eBooks from amazon.co.uk

Sick Notes / **Dr Tony Copperfield**
(ppbk, £8.99)

WELCOME TO the bizarre world of Tony Copperfield, family doctor. He spends his days fending off anxious mums, elderly sex maniacs and hopeless hypochondriacs (with his eyes peeled for the odd serious symptom). The rest of his time is taken up sparring with colleagues, battling bureaucrats and banging his head against the brick walls of the NHS.

If you've ever wondered what your GP is really thinking - and what's actually going on behind the scenes at your surgery - *SICK NOTES* is for you.

'A wonderful book, funny and insightful in equal measure'
– *Dr Phil Hammond (Private Eye's 'MD')*

'Copperfield is simply fantastic, unbelievably funny and improbably wise... everything he writes is truer than fact'
– *British Medical Journal*

'Original, funny and an incredible read' – ***The Sun***

Tony Copperfield is a Medical Journalist of the Year, has been shortlisted for UK Columnist of the Year many times and writes regularly for *The Times* and other media.

When Science Goes Wrong / **Simon LeVay**
(ppbk, £7.99)

WE LIVE in times of astonishing
scientific progress. But for every stunning
triumph there are hundreds of cock-
ups, damp squibs and disasters. Escaped
anthrax spores and nuclear explosions,
tiny data errors which send a spacecraft
hurtling to oblivion, innocent men jailed
on 'infallible' DNA evidence…just some
of the fascinating and disturbing tales
from the dark side of discovery.

**'Spine-tingling, occasionally gruesome accounts of well-
meant but disastrous scientific bungling'**
– The Los Angeles Times

'Entertaining and thought-provoking'
– Publisher's Weekly

**'The dark – but fascinating – side of science… an
absorbing read'** *– GeoTimes*

A Paramedic's Diary / **Stuart Gray**
(ppbk, £7.99)

STUART GRAY is a paramedic dealing with the worst life can throw at him. *A Paramedic's Diary* is his gripping, blow-by-blow account of a year on the streets – 12 rollercoaster months of enormous highs and tragic lows. One day he'll save a young mother's life as she gives birth, the next he might watch a young girl die on the tarmac in front of him after a hit-and-run. A gripping, entertaining and often amusing read by a talented new writer.

As heard on BBC Radio 4's Saturday Live and BBC Radio 5 Live's Donal McIntyre Show and Simon Mayo

In April 2010, Stuart Gray was named one of the country's 'best 40 bloggers' by *The Times*

***So That's Why They Call It Great Britain* / Steve Pope**
(ppbk, £7.99)

FROM THE steam engine to the jet engine to the engine of the world wide web, to vaccination and penicillin, to Viagra, chocolate bars, the flushing loo, the G&T, ibruprofen and the telephone... this is the truly astonishing story of one tiny country and its gifts to the world.

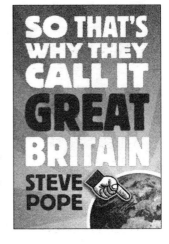

Perverting The Course Of Justice / **Inspector** Gadget
(ppbk, £7.99)

A SENIOR serving policeman picks up where PC Copperfield left off and reveals how far the insanity extends – children arrested for stealing sweets from each other while serious criminals go about their business unmolested.

'Exposes the reality of life at the sharp end'
– The Daily Telegraph

'No wonder they call us Plods... A frustrated inspector speaks out on the madness of modern policing'
– The Daily Mail

'Staggering... exposes the bloated bureaucracy that is crushing Britain' *– The Daily Express*

'You must buy this book... it is a fascinating insight'
– Kelvin MacKenzie, The Sun

In April 2010, Inspector Gadget was named
one of the country's 'best 40 bloggers' by *The Times*.